The Crux of Contrition

The Crux of Contrition

Dr. ant

Saint Norbert Media, Inc.

CONTENTS

Table of Contents

Moral Theology's Toughest Question
by
Dr. ant

The Crux of Contrition: Moral Theology's Toughest Question

Contents

Key Documents and Encyclicals

Glossary of Terms

Introduction

Catholic moral theology, deeply rooted in centuries of tradition, grapples with concepts both sublime and complex. Among these, the tension between unpardonable sins and imperfect contrition stands as a profound mystery. As we embark on this journey, we'll delve into these intricate topics, aiming to shed light on the nuanced understandings held by theologians, canon lawyers, and the Roman Catholic community.

In the shadowy corridors of history, the Sacrament of Confession has evolved, reflecting the dynamic interplay between divine grace and human frailty. Its doctrines tell a story of mercy and justice, a relentless pursuit of the penitent heart, and the ceaseless quest for absolution.

Understanding sin within Catholicism is akin to peering into a mirror that reflects our deepest imperfections. From venial to mortal sins, the nature of sin carries consequences that reverberate through the soul's eternal journey. These concepts challenge us to face the harsh realities of our own fallibility.

Saint Alphonsus Liguori emerges as a pivotal figure in our exploration. His theological framework offers a lens through which we can examine the dichotomy of contrition—perfect versus imperfect. Liguori's life and works provide context and depth to our discourse, shedding light on the stark reality and complexities of human repentance.

Our exploration is not merely historical or theoretical but deeply personal. The Sacrament of Confession, with its origins steeped in the early Church, represents a ritual passage from sin to grace. We'll traverse its evolution, the role of the priest as a representative of divine forgiveness, and the penitent's arduous journey towards reconciliation.

Forgiveness and absolution, central tenets of Catholic doctrine, hinge upon certain conditions. The process of receiving forgiveness is not a mere formality but a profound spiritual exercise requiring sincere contrition. This pathway to divine mercy is fraught with challenges, yet it's the cornerstone of the faith.

Yet, amidst the possibility of forgiveness, we encounter the chilling concept of the "unforgivable sin." Scripture and theological debate present us with different perspectives, and Liguori's insights become a guide through this perplexing territory. Can any sin be truly unforgivable, or does divine mercy transcend our understanding? This question lingers, demanding contemplation.

Imperfect contrition, often stemming from a fear of God rather than pure love, underscores humanity's struggle with true repentance. The tension between fear and love in the act of contrition brings forth a crucial aspect of our human condition. How do we reconcile these seemingly opposing motives in our journey towards God's grace?

As moral theologians, we face tough, often unsettling questions. What constitutes true repentance? Are there sins so grave that they lie beyond forgiveness? These inquiries challenge our faith and understanding, pushing us to delve deeper into the essence of contrition and mercy.

In examining historical and modern case studies of incomplete contrition, we gain insight into the real-world applications and implications of these doctrines. The role of grace in contrition, divine assistance versus free will, adds another layer of complexity to our analysis. How do we harmonize divine intervention with human responsibility?

The ecclesiastical and canonical perspectives offer a structural framework within which these theological concepts are interpreted and applied. Canon law and ecclesiastical teachings provide guidelines that inform the practice and understanding of contrition and confession within the Church.

Modern times present unique challenges to these age-old doctrines. Pastoral approaches to imperfect contrition must adapt to contemporary moral dilemmas, guiding the faithful through an ever-changing landscape while maintaining doctrinal integrity.

Finally, we turn to the concept of Divine Mercy, a beacon of hope in the midst of theological and moral complexities. The history of Divine Mercy, its associated indulgences, and its relationship to perfect and imperfect contrition reveal a pathway to reconciliation and grace that is both profound and accessible.

As we navigate these themes, we must remember that indulgences and acts of charity play a significant role in covering a multitude of sins. They serve as tangible expressions of repentance and contribute to the overall process of seeking and attaining divine mercy.

This introduction lays the foundation for our journey through Catholic moral theology, examining the interplay between sin, contrition, and forgiveness. It's an invitation to explore, question, and deepen our understanding of the faith that guides so many. The following chapters will further unravel these themes, offering insight and reflection on the path to divine reconciliation and grace.

Chapter 1: Saint Alphonsus Liguori's Theological Framework

Saint Alphonsus Liguori's theological framework is a labyrinth of meticulously crafted doctrines, designed to navigate the soul through the complexities of sin and redemption. His approach is shaped by an unwavering commitment to pastoral care and a deep understanding of human frailty. Liguori's cornerstone lies in the balance between God's justice and mercy, where he posits that even the most hardened sinner can find a path to salvation through genuine contrition. His teachings serve as a compass for moral theologians, Roman Catholics, and canon lawyers alike, meticulously balancing the rigors of doctrinal purity with the compassionate nuances of pastoral theology. The confluence of his profound insights and practical applications forms a bedrock that continues to underpin contemporary discussions on the nature and mechanics of sin, contrition, and absolution.

Early Life and Influences

The life of Saint Alphonsus Liguori begins not in obscurity but rather in the well-defined contours of a Naples that was both culturally rich and religiously intense. Born on September 27, 1696, Alphonsus came into a family that balanced its affluence with a deep sense of piety. His upbringing was a blend of rigorous scholastic training and an intense immersion in the Christian virtues. From an early age, Liguori was exposed to the moral and theological questions that would later become the cornerstone of his life's work.

From a young age, he exhibited remarkable intellectual prowess. This precocious nature was evident when Alphonsus pursued his studies under the Jesuits at the age of 13 and graduated with a doctorate in civil and canon law by 16. His intellectual formative years were spent in the cloistered environment of ecclesiastical academia, where he was first exposed to the intricacies of moral theology. These years also provided fertile ground for the philosophical influences that would later emerge in his theological frameworks.

But it wasn't just formal education that molded Alphonsus. His early life was deeply influenced by his father, Giuseppe, an officer in the Royal Navy. Giuseppe instilled in him a sense of discipline and a moral compass, albeit a stern one, which was balanced by the tender, pious influence of his mother, Anna, a model of Christian charity. This duality in his upbringing—rigorous academic instruction and a home steeped in religious devotion—prefigured the dual nature of his later theological pursuits: intense rationality melded seamlessly with fervent piety.

Despite the structured environment, Alphonsus was not isolated from the societal issues of his time. The socio-political landscape of Naples, fraught with economic disparity and moral decline, offered him a real-world theater for understanding sin and redemption. The city's melding of grandeur and squalor provided Alphonsus with an unvarnished view of human frailty, and it was among these contradictions that his compassion for the suffering began to take root.

His decision to leave a promising legal career at the age of 27, following a humiliating courtroom defeat, serves as a pivotal moment in appreciating his early influences. Disillusioned by what he perceived as corruption and moral lapse within the legal system, Alphonsus turned his sharp mind towards theology. The bite of this personal failure, combined with a spiritual vision he reportedly experienced during the incident, shifted his focus irrevocably to matters of the soul. He poured his analytical abilities into understanding Divine law and the moral imperatives that guide human behavior.

Guided by an inner call to serve the destitute, Alphonsus entered the seminary and was ordained in 1726. The years that followed saw him engaging directly with the marginalized, often walking the streets to offer solace and counsel. This pastoral work brought into sharp relief the practical applications of theology and moral judgment, compelling him to unearth solutions to the dilemmas faced by the faithful. The interaction with penitents not only strengthened his resolve but also broadened his comprehension of human guilt, shame, and the power of God's grace.

Moreover, it was during his time in seminary that he became deeply influenced by the writings of earlier theologians and saints, such as Augustine, Thomas Aquinas, and Teresa of Ávila. The works of these luminaries refined his philosophical and theological perspectives, which he would later synthesize into a cohesive theological framework. Augustine's emphasis on grace as a necessary component for human salvation and Aquinas' integration of reason and faith would become thematic pillars in Liguori's own writings.

Alphonsus was not only influenced by theological texts but also by the devotion to Marian spirituality that was prevalent in Naples. The city's deep Marian tradition, characterized by popular devotions and liturgical celebrations in honor of the Virgin Mary, left an indelible mark on him. This devotion to Mary, whom he often invoked as the Mother of Mercy, permeated his theological writings and provided a compassionate lens through which to view sin and redemption.

His deepening spirituality and theological inquiry didn't occur in an intellectual vacuum. The Catholic Church during Alphonsus' lifetime was in the throes of confrontation with Enlightenment rationalism and secularism. The Council of Trent's reforms were still being strongly felt, emphasizing the need for definitive answers to moral questions and orthodox practices. This period necessitated a robust defense of orthodox Catholicism, which deeply influenced his theological constructs. His mission, therefore, was not just academic; it was also a defense of faith under siege from the growing forces of rationalism.

In establishing the Congregation of the Most Holy Redeemer (the Redemptorists) in 1732, Alphonsus sought to extend his mission to the spiritual and material poverty he saw around him. The order's focus on preaching, teaching, and hearing confessions among the rural poor mirrored his own early pastoral encounters, further embedding in him a realpolitik approach to theology—one that is practical, compassionate, yet uncompromisingly rooted in Church doctrine.

The interplay between these myriad influences—early familial nurturing, rigorous academic training, intense personal spiritual experiences, and direct pastoral engagements—shaped a theologian primarily concerned with the human condition. Alphonsus Liguori's theological framework would thus emerge as an authentic expression of solving real-world moral dilemmas, rooted in the timeless doctrines of the Church yet imbued with a profound sense of mercy and compassion.

Key Works and Contributions

Saint Alphonsus Liguori's theological framework created an indelible mark on moral theology. One can't embark on understanding this realm without delving into his prolific contributions. Known for his numerous writings, Liguori's works have shaped the nuances of Catholic theology, particularly influencing the doctrines related to contrition and confession.

"Moral Theology" is perhaps the most pivotal of his works. This comprehensive manual, initially published in the mid-18th century, spans multiple volumes. It dives deep into the moral laws governing human behavior, with a particular focus on the sacraments, especially the Sacrament of Confession. Distinguishing between perfect and imperfect contrition, Liguori offers a detailed exposition of repentance and its necessary conditions.

Another significant contribution is his work titled "The Glories of Mary." While this may seem tangential, it directly impacts the perception of mercy and intercession within the realm of confession and absolution. Liguori's discussions on Mary as a mediator provide insights into the compassionate side of divine justice, alleviating the heavy burden that imperfect contrition can often impose on a penitent soul.

Within "The Way of the Cross," Liguori composes a devotional guide that emphasizes the contemplation of Christ's Passion. This work serves as a tool for fostering sincere remorse in believers. Through meditative prayer and reflection on Christ's sufferings, it seeks to inspire a profound sense of repentance, blending emotional depth with theological precision.

Liguori's extensive treatises on conscience and moral decision-making also merit mention. His essays and lectures underscore the importance of an informed conscience. He argues that moral decisions, whether in the confessional or in everyday life, must be guided by a well-formed conscience. This helps believers navigate the often murky waters of sin and redemption with clarity and confidence.

In "The Practice of Love of Jesus Christ," Liguori explores the interplay between love and fear in repentance. He contends that true contrition arises from the perfect love of God, rather than a fear of divine retribution. This theological stance is pivotal, shedding light on the nuanced difference between perfect and imperfect contrition, thus informing pastoral approaches to penance and forgiveness.

Furthermore, his lesser-known but impactful letters and correspondence with clerics provide a treasure trove of pastoral wisdom. These writings exhibit Liguori's practical approach to the theology of contrition and confession, offering a more personal glimpse into how he applied his theological principles in pastoral care.

Saint Alphonsus's influence extends beyond his written works to the formation of the Redemptorist congregation, which he founded. This religious order's mission emphasizes preaching the Gospel and offering the Sacrament of Confession, thereby operationalizing Liguori's theological insights into contrition and absolution. The Redemptorists carry forward his teachings, thereby perpetuating his impact on moral theology.

One cannot overlook Liguori's role in the debates and reforms of the Church's approach to moral theology. Often at odds with rigorists of his time, he championed a more lenient approach to penance that didn't compromise on the necessity of contrition but allowed for divine mercy's generous application. This balancing act between justice and mercy has deeply influenced contemporary Catholic doctrinal stances.

Liguori's contributions aren't limited to theological academia; they permeate church praxis at every level. His guidelines on how priests should administer the Sacrament of Confession, found in works like "Selva, or a Collection of Materials for Ecclesiastical Retreats," remain valuable resources for clergy seeking to offer effective and compassionate pastoral care.

His poetry and hymns, while not strictly theological treatises, also enrich our understanding of his spiritual vision. Works like "Tu Scendi Dalle Stelle" reveal his emotive and devotional side, helping to cultivate a sense of reverence and penitence among the faithful. This artistic contribution complements his theological writings, offering a multi-faceted approach to understanding sin, contrition, and divine grace.

Alphonsus Liguori's theological inquiries also delve into apologetics, defending the Catholic doctrine of contrition and confession against Protestant criticisms. His polemical works serve not only as defenses of Catholic orthodoxy but also as clarifications and expositions that help refine the Church's own understanding and teaching on these critical subjects.

It's essential to note his influence on subsequent theologians and church councils. His works were cited in various Vatican documents and continue to be required reading in seminaries. His theological principles resonate in the writings of later moral theologians and continue to inform contemporary debates on the nature of sin and repentance.

"Doctrine, Morals, and Spirituality" is another subsequent compilation where Liguori systematically arranges his theological, moral, and spiritual insights into one coherent framework. This structured presentation offers an invaluable resource for understanding the interconnectedness of his theological vision, particularly concerning contrition and the sacramental life.

Lastly, his personal piety, reflected in his devotional practices and writings, provides a model for both clergy and laity. His emphasis on habitual prayer, examination of conscience, and frequent reception of the sacraments underscores the importance he placed on fostering a continuous state of repentance and spiritual readiness.

In summary, Saint Alphonsus Liguori's key works and contributions form a vast, intricate tapestry that underpins Catholic moral theology. His profound insights into contrition, confession, and absolution continue to guide the faithful and the clergy alike, fostering a deeper understanding of God's boundless mercy and the path to true repentance.

Chapter 2: Concepts of Sin in Catholicism

The Catholic understanding of sin is a nuanced tapestry woven with the threads of mortal and venial sins, each carrying its own weight and consequence. Mortal sins, grave in matter and fully consented, sever one's relationship with God and demand reconciliation through confession. Venial sins, while straining this divine connection, do not break it entirely and are often seen as moral missteps that require spiritual attention and growth. The nature of sin in Catholic doctrine is intrinsically tied to the intentions and awareness of the sinner, highlighting a complex interplay between human free will and divine judgment. As we navigate this theological landscape, it becomes evident that not all sins bear equal gravity, nor do they entail uniform consequences, compelling a deeper exploration of the personal and communal dimensions of sin within the faith. The consequences of sin, therefore, extend beyond eternal separation or purification, influencing one's earthly journey and the Church's sacramental life. This complexity necessitates a thorough investigation into contrition, absolution, and the role of divine grace, forming the cornerstone of Catholic moral theology.

Venial vs. Mortal Sins

In the nuanced field of moral theology, the distinction between venial and mortal sins forms a cornerstone of Catholic thought. This dichotomy isn't merely a matter of severity but also explores the degree to which a sin ruptures one's relationship with God. Venial sins are lesser sins that weaken, but do not sever, the connection with divine grace. Conversely, mortal sins are grave offenses that entirely break one's relationship with God, aligning the soul with eternal damnation unless absolved through the Sacrament of Confession.

The foundation for this classification finds its roots in the Bible, specifically in the First Letter of John, which distinguishes between sins that lead to death and those that do not (1 John 5:16-17). The Church Fathers and subsequent theologians elaborated on this, adding layers of doctrinal clarity. St. Augustine, for instance, categorized sins based on their effect on the soul's journey towards God. Later, Thomas Aquinas crystalized the distinctions further by examining the intent and nature of the act, elucidating the criteria that render a sin either venial or mortal.

A mortal sin, by its nature, achieves three conditions: it must be of grave matter, committed with full knowledge, and performed with deliberate consent. The gravity of the act is generally defined by the

Ten Commandments; offenses such as murder, adultery, and theft fall squarely into this category. When a person, fully aware of the sinful nature of their actions, commits a grave act with unambiguous intentionality, the bond with divine grace is fractured. In contrast, venial sins come about through lesser matters or grave matters carried out without full knowledge or consent. These sins, although damaging, don't put the soul in peril of eternal separation from God.

Consider, for instance, an inadvertent lie to avoid minor inconvenience versus a calculated deceit intending to cause significant harm. The former is typically venial, given its minor nature and potentially spur-of-the-moment origin. The latter, however, veers towards mortal sin due to its grievous nature and premeditated intention.

One might wonder about the moral culpability during periods of impaired judgment. Catholic theology acknowledges that mitigating factors like fear, ignorance, and coercion can affect one's responsibility. This acknowledgment doesn't excuse the sin but shifts its gravity. In such instances, the Church urges proper spiritual direction to illuminate conscience and foster sincere contrition.

The history of this differentiation also has significant pastoral implications. Understanding the nuances helps priests guide their congregations more effectively, particularly in the confessional. Evaluating the state of the penitent's soul relies on the awareness of these categories. A penitent struggling with repetitive venial sins may receive distinct pastoral advice aimed at strengthening their will and moral resolve. Meanwhile, someone confessing a mortal sin will encounter a more robust spiritual intervention focused on repentance and absolution.

In the Sacrament of Confession, the acknowledgment of mortal sins is imperative for absolution. The penitent must confess all known mortal sins in kind and number to restore sanctifying grace. Venial sins, although not strictly required to be confessed, are encouraged to be mentioned as a measure of spiritual growth and humility. By confessing venial sins, the faithful expose themselves to sacramental grace, fortifying their resistance to future temptations.

Yet, there exists a grey area where sins seem to straddle the line between venial and mortal. Such ambiguities often perplex even seasoned confessors. Here, the intention behind the act becomes pivotal. Take, for example, omissions—failures to perform acts known to be required. If the omission involves neglecting a grave duty knowingly and willingly, it could potentially bear the weight of mortal sin. However, a lapse due to inadvertence or circumstantial inability might be deemed venial.

The theological and pastoral aspects surrounding venial and mortal sins extend into everyday Catholic practice. Priests are trained to recognize these subtleties and address them during confession. They play an instrumental role in educating the faithful about their moral responsibilities and the repercussions of their actions. The sacraments, especially Confession and Eucharist, serve as critical points of contact where the faithful constantly reassess their moral standing and seek divine aid.

The distinction also emphasizes the importance of continual moral vigilance. Venial sins, while not mortal, are not benign. Repeated venial sins can predispose a soul towards mortal sin, acting as a slippery slope. This progression underscores the necessity of regular self-examination and spiritual direction. Priests often encourage frequent confession not just for the absolution of mortal sins but as a means to maintain spiritual health against the corrosion of venial sins.

Pondering the theological underpinnings, it becomes evident that the concept of sin extends beyond mere rule-following. It embodies the relational aspect between the individual and God. Mortal sins are seen as direct rejections of God's love, while venial sins represent minor lapses in that relationship. Understanding these distinctions aids the faithful in cultivating a life aligned with divine precepts, ultimately aspiring towards sanctity.

Moreover, this dichotomy influences how the faithful approach the Eucharist. Conscious avoidance of mortal sin is fundamental before partaking in the Holy Communion. The Eucharist, known as the "Sacrament of Love," demands a state of grace, free of grave sin. On the other hand, venial sins, while less severe, still require the penitent's acknowledgment and intent for amendment. Participating in the Eucharist can cleanse venial sins by virtue of its sacramental grace, thus reiterating the interconnectedness of these practices within the Church's spiritual framework.

Historically, the Church has seen shifts in how these distinctions are taught and understood. Earlier ecclesiastical edicts imposed stringent penalties for mortal sins, leading to rigorous penance. The evolution towards a more compassionate pastoral approach shows a balance between upholding doctrinal truth and extending mercy. This evolution is pivotal in how venial and mortal sins are viewed by modern Catholics, encompassing both doctrinal fidelity and pastoral care.

In summation, the Catholic doctrines on venial and mortal sins are not archaic relics but vibrant guides for moral and spiritual life. They remind the faithful of their connection to God, urging conversion and vigilance. By demarcating sins into these categories, the Church provides a pathway for sincere repentance, spiritual growth, and ultimately, eternal union with God. The exploration of these themes is essential for moral theologians, canon lawyers, and practitioners of the faith, ensuring a deeper comprehension of sin's complexities and the boundless scope of divine mercy.

The Nature of Sin and Its Consequences

In Catholic teaching, the nature of sin is anchored deeply within the theological and moral doctrines of the Church, a complex network of ideas that has been scrutinized and elaborated upon for centuries. Sin, in essence, is a fundamental disruption of one's relationship with God. This disruption manifests not merely as a series of moral failures but as a profound rupture within the very soul, alienating it from divine grace.

Sin is traditionally divided into two main categories: venial and mortal. Mortal sin constitutes a grave matter, committed with full knowledge and deliberate consent, which ruptures the sanctifying grace in a person's soul. Venial sin, on the other hand, involves less serious matters and does not fully sever one's relationship with God but weakens it nonetheless. The distinctions are not just theological but practical, affecting how one approaches repentance and receives absolution.

The consequences of sin reverberate beyond the individual. Within the communal context of the Church, sin affects not just the sinner but the entire body of believers. This communal dimension reinforces the need for public confession and penance, integrating both individual contrition and communal restitution.

One must also consider the concept of original sin, which underscores the human inclination towards wrongdoing inherited from Adam and Eve. This innate propensity necessitates divine grace for redemption, highlighting the indispensable role of Jesus Christ's sacrificial act. The tempests of everyday temptations and failings bring to light the fragile nature of human morality, constantly needing divine guidance.

In exploring the consequences of sin, it becomes imperative to delve into both the temporal and eternal ramifications. Temporal consequences might include spiritual malaise, psychological guilt, and social alienation. In contrast, eternal consequences touch upon the very essence of salvation and damnation, underscoring the gravity of mortal sin and the path to redemption through contrition and confession.

Venial sins, while less severe, still bear consequences that should not be underestimated. They might lead to vices becoming habitual, thus leaving the soul more susceptible to mortal sin. Moreover, repeatedly disregarding the gravity of venial sins can harden the heart, making genuine contrition more challenging.

The theological framework offered by figures such as Saint Alphonsus Liguori provides a comprehensive understanding of these intricate layers. His writings emphasize that no sin is beyond the reach of God's mercy if approached with true contrition. However, the sinner's heart must align with divine will, recognizing the gravity of their transgressions.

The path to reconciliation is paved with acknowledgment and remorse, but it's not an easy road. The Church teaches that true repentance requires not just a verbal admission but a deep, interior conversion of heart. This conversion involves recognizing the full weight of one's sins and making a sincere effort to amend one's life.

One striking consequence of mortal sin is spiritual death, a term that captures the severance from God's sanctifying grace. This is a stark contrast to the life of grace that the Church encourages. The Catechism of the Catholic Church provides an elucidating guideline: "Sin is before all else an offense against God, a rupture of communion with him" (CCC 1440). This rupture is what leads to the necessity of the Sacrament of Confession to restore one's state of grace.

Mortal sin, when committed, needs the intentional act of seeking God's forgiveness through confession. The confessional is not just a symbolic act but a spiritual clinic where wounds are examined and healed beneath the tender care of a priest. The role of the priest is crucial, acting in persona Christi, binding and loosing sins through the authority given by Christ Himself.

The mystery and severity of sin underscore the indispensable role of divine grace in the economy of salvation. The Church, in her wisdom, has developed a sacramental system to aid the faithful in their journey toward holiness. Baptism initially cleanses the stain of original sin, but the Sacrament of Reconciliation provides repeated opportunity for the healing of post-baptismal sin.

Yet, the conversation cannot stop at doctrinal explanations; it must also encompass personal reflection and a constant striving toward moral improvement. Sin's consequences serve as a sobering reminder of the potential distance from God that one's actions can create. They call for a vigilant moral conscience, regular examination of self, and the sacraments as channels of grace.

The Church's history teems with the lives of saints who deeply understood the nature of sin and its catastrophic potential. Saints like Augustine and Thomas Aquinas grappled with these theological and moral intricacies, offering timeless insights. Their writings serve as both a warning and a guide, helping the faithful navigate the treacherous waters of sin and repentance.

Finally, understanding the consequences of sin reminds the Catholic faithful of the profound love and mercy of God. Despite the heavy weight of sin, God's grace always offers a way back. This divine mercy does not trivialize sin but illuminates the path toward redemption, reflecting the loving nature of a God who desires not the death of a sinner but their return to righteousness.

- Recognition of mortality and veniality.
- Consequences are both temporal and eternal.
- Sin impacts both individual and communal aspects.
- Restoration through the Sacrament of Confession.

In conclusion, the nature of sin and its consequences in Catholicism form a complex narrative of moral failure and hope for redemption. These themes will continue to resonate through the subsequent chapters, offering deeper insight into contrition, confession, and the many layers that define the journey towards divine grace.

Chapter 3: The Doctrine of Contrition

In the intricate tapestry of Catholic doctrine, contrition stands as a central pillar, a concept that delicately balances the themes of divine mercy and human frailty. Perfect contrition—sorrow for sins arising from pure love of God—has its roots deeply entwined with theological ideals, presenting a sanctified path towards reconciliation. Imperfect contrition, on the other hand, dwells in the murky waters of fear and self-interest, where remorse stems from dread of divine punishment rather than genuine love. The historical development of contrition doctrine reveals a nuanced journey, as Church teachings evolved to encapsulate both divine justice and mercy. Through ecclesiastical debate and scriptural interpretation, the Church has endeavored to clarify the conditions under which contrition is deemed sufficient for absolution, acknowledging that imperfect contrition, while less noble, still opens a pathway to divine forgiveness. The tension between these forms of contrition foregrounds much of the theological discussion on sin and redemption, reflecting a divine pedagogy that seeks to gradually elevate the human heart from fear to love.

Perfect Contrition

To understand perfect contrition, one must first look deep into the essence of contrition itself. At its core, perfect contrition is born from a profound and genuine love for God, surpassing the fear of punishment. It represents the contrite heart fully aware of God's infinite goodness and mercy, leading the penitent to sorrow that transcends mere dread of consequences.

This profound contrition, often described in theological terms as "contritio perfecta," creates a distinct, almost mystic awareness of one's sins against Divine Love. It is essential for mortal sins to be forgiven even in the absence of formal confession, provided the intent to receive the sacrament at the earliest opportunity remains. This doctrine forms the bedrock of Catholic teachings on the subject and echoes through the centuries of ecclesiastical thought.

Perfect contrition isn't an easily achieved state. It requires a deep spiritual alignment and a heart entirely oriented towards God. The Church Fathers, including Saint Alphonsus Liguori, highlighted that such a pure form of contrition is not merely an emotional repentance but a profound act of the will. This act springs from an elevated understanding of God's love and a recognition of our sins as wounds upon that love.

Consider the words of Saint Augustine, who described a contrite heart as one where love for God suffuses every thought and action, thus evolving mere regret into transcendent sorrow. It was Liguori, however, who systematized these ideas into a coherent theological framework that has informed Catholic teachings since his era.

In practical terms, the Church hasn't left the faithful to wander alone in pursuing perfect contrition. Through the ages, various devotions and practices have been recommended—prayer, meditation on the Passion, the Rosary, and devout reading of Sacred Scripture. These are spiritual tools aimed at cultivating a heart capable of perfect contrition.

One might wonder why this emphasis on perfect contrition is so crucial. It boils down to the relationship between sin, contrition, and absolution. Mortal sins sever our connection with God, and perfect contrition restores it in a way imperfect contrition cannot. While imperfect contrition—motivated by fear of divine justice—is acceptable, perfect contrition signifies a more profound reconciliation, a personal return to the fold of Divine Love.

The journey to perfect contrition also involves a paradox. It is simultaneously an act of divine grace and human will. The Church teaches that while divine grace initiates and sustains all holy movements in the soul, human freedom must respond willingly. This interplay between grace and free will is part of the great mystery of contrition and forgiveness.

In light of historical development, the Council of Trent emphasized the indispensable value of perfect contrition. This council, considered a vital moment in the shaping of Catholic doctrine, reaffirmed that perfect contrition reconciles us with God before we even approach the confessional. This doctrine was not merely speculative theology; it offered pastoral assurance, especially in instances where immediate confession to a priest wasn't possible.

Liguori delved into this concept with a meticulousness that reflected his dedication to moral theology. He argued that understanding perfect contrition requires not only theological study but a heart attuned to God's love—a divine gift beyond human calculation. His treatises on contrition have become reference points for moral theologians and remain integral to catechetical instruction.

An example from the annals of Church history underscores the significance of this doctrine. During the devastating plagues of the Middle Ages, the reality of sudden death without the benefit of confession loomed large. The faithful were encouraged to cultivate perfect contrition to ensure their souls were not lost, even if they couldn't reach a priest. Here, perfect contrition was more than a theological concept—it was a spiritual lifeline.

Nonetheless, achieving perfect contrition is not a task one accomplishes through sheer effort. It is the Holy Spirit who moves the heart towards that purity of repentance. Hence, the Church advocates for constant engagement in sacramental life, continuous prayer, and acts of charity. These practices condition the soul to be more receptive to perfect contrition.

Indeed, the theological exploration of perfect contrition doesn't negate the importance of the Sacrament of Confession. Rather, it enhances our understanding of its necessity. While perfect contrition reconciles us with God, confession to a priest provides the sacramental grace to support and sustain our spiritual journey.

In this dynamic dance between divine justice and mercy, perfect contrition emerges as a luminous beacon. It guides the penitent soul towards a heartfelt return to God, away from the darkness of sin. As theologians and canon lawyers unravel the intricacies of Church doctrine, they unearth treasures like this—doctrines that speak to the heart's deepest yearnings for reconciliation and divine love.

Perfect contrition, therefore, is not just an academic subject confined to theological treatises. It is a living doctrine, pulsating with the heartbeat of God's mercy, accessible to every penitent heart. Its profound implications stretch from the pages of sacred tradition to the quiet prayers of the faithful, knitting them together in a divine tapestry of redemption.

Imperfect Contrition

Imperfect contrition, also known as attrition, occupies a complex and nuanced space within the doctrine of contrition in Catholic theology. It is the sorrow for sin driven more by fear of divine retribution—hell and eternal separation from God—than by pure love of God. While the Church holds perfect contrition as the ideal form of repentance, where sorrow arises out of love for God, imperfect contrition is nonetheless significant and has its own theological implications.

Acknowledging human frailty, the Church teaches that imperfect contrition, while not perfect, still holds value. It reflects a genuine fear of God and acknowledges His supreme authority. Though motivated by a more self-centered fear of punishment, this kind of sorrow still opens the penitent to God's mercy. In the sacrament of confession, imperfect contrition, coupled with a firm purpose of amendment, suffices for the forgiveness of sins. Thus, the Church demonstrates a profound understanding of human nature, where even imperfect steps toward penitence are validated in light of divine mercy.

The tension between unforgivable sins and imperfect contrition introduces a fascinating exploration of the justice and mercy of God. Certain sins, characterized as "unforgivable," spark heated theological debate, primarily due to their gravity and seemingly absolute nature. Jesus' words in the Gospels about the sin against the Holy Spirit provoke intense scrutiny and interpretation. Within this framework, imperfect contrition's role becomes even more vital, for it can guide souls away from such despair.

Historically, the doctrine of contrition has undergone considerable development, reflecting the Church's pastoral wisdom and deepening theological insights. Impelled by the theological works of early Church Fathers and further articulated during the scholastic period, imperfect contrition's acceptance marks a significant pastoral concern for the salvation of souls. Theologians like Saint Thomas Aquinas and the Council of Trent further clarified that imperfect contrition, stemming from fear of punishment rather than perfect love, remains valuable.

This evolution indicates the Church's adaptive approach, balancing strict doctrine with pastoral care.

Rome's historic cobblestones have witnessed countless souls traversing from imperfect contrition to a fuller understanding and love of God. The sacrament of confession serves as a vessel for this transformation. In the dim chambers of confessionals, priests provide not only absolution but also spiritual guidance, encouraging penitents to grow in their contrition, moving from fear to love.

Delving deeper into imperfect contrition, one must consider the psychological and spiritual dimensions involved. The phenomenon is rooted in the existential realities of fear, guilt, and the hope for redemption. Every sinner, in his or her unique journey, may start with a keen awareness of divine judgment and evolve into a purer form of repentance characterized by love for God. This dynamic, while deeply personal, finds its expression and resolution in the structured practice of sacramental confession.

Saint Alphonsus Liguori, a towering figure in moral theology, intricately analyzes contrition in his writings. He affirms that imperfect contrition, though not as elevated as perfect contrition, is still acceptable and effective in the economy of salvation. Saint Alphonsus' perspective helps bridge the apparent chasm between human weakness and divine perfection, illustrating God's willingness to work through our imperfections. His works highlight how even the initial spark of fear can ignite a more profound transformation within the soul.

In contemporary pastoral settings, clergy are frequently confronted with penitents who naturally exhibit imperfect contrition. This reality underscores the importance of compassionate, patient guidance, emphasizing that the Church does not demand instant perfection but promotes a journey toward spiritual maturity. Confessors are trained to recognize the beginnings of divine fear and to nurture it towards divine love, integrating theological principles with pastoral sensitivity.

Theologically, the essence of imperfect contrition lies in its openness to grace. Even though it stems from fear of punishment, it demonstrates a recognition of God's justice and the heinousness of sin. Thus, it positions the penitent as receptive to the grace dispensed through the sacrament of confession. This receptivity is crucial, for through grace, the divine offers assistance in transforming the initial fear-based contrition into something richer and more love-centered.

The complexity of imperfect contrition also invites reflection on the nature of God's mercy. How can a just and merciful God look favorably upon a contrition that is, by definition, flawed? The answer resides in the overarching narrative of divine love and mercy, which envelops even the imperfect steps taken by humanity. The sacrament of confession becomes a tableau where God's justice and mercy merge, allowing imperfect contrition to be perfected over time through ongoing conversion and deeper spiritual life.

Imperfect contrition does not stand alone but interacts dynamically with other theological concepts such as penance, grace, and the sacramental life. The process of repentance and reconciliation is multifaceted, where initial fear-induced sorrow acts as a catalyst for a more profound conversion. The Church's recognition of this multifaceted reality ensures that no penitent is left without hope, and every genuine effort toward repentance finds a place within the divine economy of salvation.

From a canonical perspective, the role of imperfect contrition stands affirmed within the Code of Canon Law, providing clear guidelines for its adequacy in sacramental confession. This codification emphasizes the universality and consistency of the Church's approach to sin and repentance, ensuring that theological principles are rigorously applied and pastorally implemented.

Moving beyond individual recognition, imperfect contrition also holds communal significance. It reflects the Church's mission to seek and save the lost, embodying Christ's parable of the Good Shepherd. Every act of imperfect contrition signifies a step taken by a member of Christ's flock towards reconciling with God, underscoring the communal journey towards holiness.

In conclusion, imperfect contrition, with its roots deep in the human experience of fear and reverence, is an essential aspect of the Catholic doctrine of contrition. It is a testament to the Church's understanding of human nature and its pastoral commitment to guiding souls toward ultimate reconciliation with God. Imperfect though it may be, this form of contrition is imbued with divine potential, promising transformation through the sacramental life. The Church's wisdom, as articulated by saints, theologians, and canon lawyers, confirms that even amidst imperfection, there lies a path to divine love and mercy.

Historical Development

The doctrine of contrition has undergone significant evolution over the centuries, shaped by theological, cultural, and ecclesiastical changes. To understand this progression, one must venture back to the early Christian communities where the seeds of this doctrine were planted. Initially, contrition was not as clearly defined as it is today; it was a more intuitive concept rooted in repentance and the desire for reconciliation with God.

In the early church, penance was a public affair. Christians who committed grave sins were required to confess their sins openly before the congregation, an act that underscored the seriousness of their transgression and their sincere remorse. This public form of penance was both a deterrent for others and a humbling experience for the penitent, ensuring that contrition was genuine and not merely a superficial display.

Over time, the institution of private confession began to gain traction. This transition was largely in response to practical and pastoral concerns. As Christianity spread, the number of converts increased, and it became impractical to maintain the rigor of public penance. Private confession allowed priests to address the spiritual needs of individual penitents more effectively, ensuring that contrition remained a personal and introspective process.

The fourth and fifth centuries brought further developments. St. Augustine of Hippo, a towering figure in Christian theology, played a pivotal role in shaping the church's understanding of sin and contrition. Augustine's emphasis on the internal state of the soul rather than external acts of penance marked a significant shift. Genuine contrition, according to Augustine, required an inner transformation and a sincere turning away from sin, prompted by love of God rather than fear of punishment.

This nuanced view of contrition continued to evolve through the medieval period. The penitential system became more structured, culminating in the establishment of the sacrament of confession as a formal and essential practice for all Christians. The Fourth Lateran Council in 1215 codified this by making annual confession obligatory for all baptized Christians. This move towards formalization necessitated a clearer distinction between perfect and imperfect contrition.

Perfect contrition, motivated by love for God, became the ideal. Yet, imperfect contrition, driven by the fear of hell and divine justice, was not dismissed; it was seen as a stepping stone towards perfect contrition. The church recognized that the journey to spiritual perfection often began with less than perfect motivations but could lead to profound internal transformation.

The scholastic period further refined these distinctions. Thomas Aquinas, one of the most influential theologians of the medieval church, articulated a comprehensive theology of contrition. He reinforced the idea that contrition was primarily an act of the will, driven by the intellect's recognition of sin's gravity and the heart's movement towards sorrow. Aquinas' synthesis of reason and faith provided a robust framework that guided subsequent theological discussions on the topic.

The Council of Trent in the 16th century marked another pivotal moment in the historical development of contrition. In response to the challenges posed by the Protestant Reformation, the Council reaffirmed the importance of the sacrament of confession and the necessity of contrition for the remission of sins. Trent emphasized that while perfect contrition could remit sins outside of confession, imperfect contrition required the sacrament for absolution. This doctrinal clarity was essential in countering Protestant critiques and ensuring theological consistency within the Catholic Church.

Post-Trent, the church continued to deepen its understanding of contrition through various papal encyclicals and theological treatises. The writings of Saint Alphonsus Liguori in the 18th century are particularly noteworthy. Liguori's pastoral sensitivity and theological rigor provided valuable insights into the practical aspects of contrition. He stressed that while perfect contrition was desirable, God's grace could elevate imperfect contrition to a state where it was sufficient for absolution when paired with the sacrament of confession.

In the modern era, the Second Vatican Council brought renewed attention to the sacrament of confession and the doctrine of contrition. The council's pastoral approach sought to reconnect the faithful with the sacrament by highlighting God's mercy and love. This period witnessed a shift from a juridical understanding of confession to a more relational and therapeutic model. The emphasis was on healing and reconciliation, reflecting the church's response to contemporary spiritual and psychological needs.

As moral theologians and canon lawyers delved into the implications of contrition in an increasingly complex world, debates arose concerning the nature of sin, culpability, and the conditions for forgiveness. These discussions were not merely academic but had profound pastoral implications, particularly in guiding penitents towards genuine repentance and spiritual growth.

Technological advancements and cultural shifts in the 20th and 21st centuries have also influenced the church's approach to contrition. The digital age, with its new forms of communication and ethical dilemmas, presents fresh challenges for the doctrine. Nonetheless, the church adapts, seeking to remain relevant while upholding the timeless principles of contrition and reconciliation.

Throughout its historical development, the doctrine of contrition has been a dynamic and evolving concept, reflecting the church's attempt to balance divine justice with mercy. From the early days of public penance to the intimate sacrament of confession, the journey has been one of deepening understanding and pastoral care. As we move forward, this rich history serves as a foundation, guiding the faithful in their pursuit of true contrition and reconciliation with God.

Chapter 4: The Sacrament of Confession

In the dimly lit confines of the confessional, where whispered secrets are exchanged, lies the cornerstone of Catholic penitential practice: the Sacrament of Confession. This sacramental rite, having evolved from the early Christian penitential practices, permits the penitent to unburden their soul while seeking divine forgiveness. Across the centuries, the role of the priest has crystallized, serving as both guide and judge, whose power to absolve stems not from personal merit but from the sacramental grace of Holy Orders. Central to this sacred transaction is the penitent's inner journey—a pilgrimage marked by humility, sorrow, and a fervent resolve to amend one's life. Here, imperfect contrition, often driven by fear of eternal damnation, paradoxically meets the boundless mercy of God, embodying a delicate interplay between divine justice and mercy. The confessional's hallowed dialogues thus remain an enduring testament to the Church's unwavering belief in the potential for redemption and the transformative power of grace.

Origins and Evolution

The history of the Catholic Church is a tapestry woven from threads of tradition, doctrine, and evolving practices. The Sacrament of Confession, formally referred to as the Sacrament of Penance or Reconciliation, is one such thread. Its origins and development mirror the Church's response to human frailty and divine mercy, offering a lens into the theological shifts and pastoral concerns of the past two millennia.

The roots of this sacrament can be traced back to the early Christian community, where the concept of forgiveness was already integral to the nascent faith. In the Gospels, Jesus is depicted as forgiving sins, a divine prerogative that He extended to His apostles. "Whose sins you forgive are forgiven them, and whose sins you retain are retained" (John 20:23). This scriptural foundation established the authority of the Church to forgive sins, a cornerstone on which the sacrament would be built.

Initially, the forgiveness of sins was a communal affair. Early Christians confessed their transgressions publicly, in the presence of the ecclesial community, reflecting a profound sense of corporate solidarity. This practice, however, was daunting and often left penitents stigmatized. Over time, as the Church grew and diversified, the need for a more private and pastoral approach became evident.

By the 3rd century, the role of the clergy in administering penance started to take shape, with bishops and priests assuming the responsibility. A significant milestone in the evolution of the Sacrament of Confession was the introduction of the "penitential books" or "libri poenitentiales" in the early medieval period. These texts provided guidelines for assigning penances based on the severity of sins, standardizing the process and ensuring a measure of fairness and consistency.

The Celtic monks, particularly in Ireland, played a pivotal role in transforming the practice of confession. They pioneered the concept of "private" or "auricular" confession—confession made in private to a priest. This innovation, driven by monastic pastoral care, facilitated frequent and repeatable access to the sacrament, promoting a more personalized and introspective approach to repentance.

By the 6th century, private confession began to spread to the European mainland. The Fourth Lateran Council of 1215 codified this practice by mandating annual confession for all Christians. This decree aligned with the Church's increasing institutional framework, necessitated by the complexities of administering a growing and diverse flock.

The sacrament underwent further refinement during the Scholastic period. Theologians like Thomas Aquinas provided rigorous theological underpinnings, articulating the sacrament's efficacy and mechanics. Aquinas emphasized the necessity of contrition, confession, and satisfaction—the "three acts of the penitent"—and elucidated the role of the priest as a judge and healer. These theological developments solidified the understanding of the sacrament not just as a juridical act but as a process of spiritual healing.

Following the Protestant Reformation, the Council of Trent (1545–1563) addressed the Sacrament of Confession with a renewed sense of urgency. In response to Protestant critiques, which often rejected or minimized the necessity of confession to a priest, the Council reaffirmed its indispensability. Trent articulated the theology of confession in terms of divine justice and mercy, emphasizing the sacrament's role in restoring the penitent to God's grace.

The post-Tridentine era saw a significant push towards uniformity and instruction. The Roman Catechism, issued in the wake of Trent, served as a definitive guide for priests and laypeople alike. It detailed the correct procedures for confession and underscored the importance of proper disposition, thus influencing pastoral practice across the globe. The sacrament's accessibility was further enhanced by the establishment of confessionals in churches, providing a designated, private space for the rite.

Throughout the modern era, the Sacrament of Confession continued to evolve, especially in the wake of Vatican II (1962–1965). The council sought to renew the sacrament's pastoral efficacy by encouraging greater emphasis on reconciliation and less on juridical aspects. This shift reflected the council's broader focus on aggiornamento, or "bringing up to date," and the need to address contemporary spiritual needs. Liturgical reforms included the introduction of communal penance services and the option for general absolution under specific conditions, though private confession remained the normative practice.

Modern canonical and theological discussions further refined the sacrament's application. Canon law emphasized the secrecy of the confessional, enshrining the absolute inviolability of the sacramental seal. This protection underscores the Church's commitment to the penitent's dignity and privacy, fostering an atmosphere of trust that is crucial for genuine contrition and confession.

The question of imperfect contrition, or attrition, remains a challenging aspect of the sacrament's theology. While perfect contrition, motivated purely by love of God, is ideal, the Church acknowledges that imperfect contrition—often prompted by fear of divine punishment—can also suffice if coupled with the sacramental act. This nuanced understanding reflects the Church's pastoral sensitivity, recognizing human complexities while upholding the sacrament's sanctity.

The Sacrament of Confession, thus, stands as a testament to the Church's enduring mission to mediate divine mercy. Its evolution is marked by a delicate balance between doctrinal rigor and pastoral compassion, responding to the faithful's need for spiritual healing and redemption. As moral theologians, canon lawyers, and devout Catholics continue to engage with its rich heritage, they uncover layers of meaning and grace that inform both personal piety and communal faith.

In conclusion, the story of the Sacrament of Confession is one of transformation and continuity. From its early communal roots to its private, introspective practice today, the sacrament has adapted to the changing contours of Christian life. Its origins in Christ's ministry, its development through medieval scholasticism, and its refinement in response to modern challenges all speak to the Church's unwavering dedication to guiding souls towards reconciliation and salvation.

The Role of the Priest

The priest stands as an essential figure in the Sacrament of Confession, functioning not merely as an intermediary between the penitent and God, but as a shepherd guiding his flock through the complex terrain of sin and redemption. This role encompasses various dimensions — spiritual, legal, and pastoral — each grounded in centuries of theological development and ecclesiastical tradition. The priest's responsibilities are anchored in the power vested in him through the sacrament of Holy Orders, which grants him the divine authority to absolve sins.

At the heart of the priest's role is the act of absolution. Absolution is not just a simple pronouncement of forgiveness, but a sacramental act that brings about a true spiritual transformation. The priest, through the authority given to him by Christ and the Church, pronounces the words of absolution: "I absolve you from your sins in the name of the Father, and of the Son, and of the Holy Spirit." This act signifies the direct involvement of God's mercy, mediated through the priest, effectively restoring the penitent to a state of grace. The gravity and solemnity of these words underscore the priest's profound role.

The priest must also be adept in moral theology, possessing the wisdom to discern the nature of the penitent's sins and to provide counsel that guides them towards true contrition and amendment of life. This aspect of the priest's role requires both intellectual rigor and deep spiritual insight. He must weigh the penitent's confession, distinguishing between venial and mortal sins, and understanding the degrees of culpability. This discernment is not merely academic but deeply pastoral, aimed at aiding the penitent in achieving genuine repentance and spiritual growth.

In addition to absolution, the priest fulfills a judicial role within the confessional. He must judge the sincerity of the penitent's contrition, which could be either perfect or imperfect. The penitent's intention to sin no more and their disposition towards reconciliation with God are also scrutinized. This involves a delicate balance of justice and mercy, where the priest must be firm yet compassionate, aiming always at the penitent's reconciliation with God.

Guidance and penance are integral to the priest's function. Penance serves a dual purpose: it acts as a remedy for the spiritual damage caused by sin and as a preventive measure against future transgressions. The priest, therefore, prescribes suitable penances that reflect the nature and gravity of the sin, guiding the penitent's journey back to righteousness. This instructional role ties closely to the pastoral care he must offer, ensuring that the penance prescribed leads to a genuine conversion of heart and mind.

Moreover, the priest's role extends beyond the confessional booth. He is responsible for creating an environment that fosters a culture of frequent confession and repentance within the community. This involves preaching on the importance of the sacrament, educating the faithful about sin and contrition, and being available and approachable for confessions. By doing so, the priest helps to cultivate a community that remains continually aware of its need for God's mercy and actively seeks it.

The priest must be a beacon of discretion and confidentiality. The seal of confession is inviolable, meaning that anything revealed during confession can never be disclosed by the priest. This absolute confidentiality ensures that the penitent can speak freely and honestly without fear of their sins being exposed. The inviolability of the confessional seal is a testament to the sacred trust placed in priests and highlights the gravity of their role as confidants and spiritual advisors.

Historically, the role of the priest in confession has evolved alongside the Church's understanding of sin and penance. In the early centuries of the Church, public penance was the norm for grave sins, but over time, the practice shifted towards private confession to a priest. This transition speaks to the Church's growing emphasis on personal pastoral care and the therapeutic value of the sacrament. The priest, therefore, acts both as a healer of souls and a guardian of ecclesiastical discipline.

The priest's interaction with the penitent is indelibly marked by the theological understanding of God as both just and merciful. This duality calls the priest to emulate these divine attributes in his ministry. He must balance the demands of justice, which require a sincere confession and genuine contrition, with the call for mercy, which seeks to restore the penitent to God's grace. This balance is not easily achieved and demands a profound spiritual maturity and pastoral sensitivity from the priest.

Furthermore, the priest must often navigate the complexities of imperfect contrition, where the penitent's sorrow for sin is motivated more by fear of hell than by love of God. Here, the priest's role becomes even more nuanced. He must guide the penitent towards a deeper understanding and experience of divine love, encouraging a shift from fear to love as the motivation for repentance. This transformative journey from imperfect to perfect contrition is profoundly pastoral and requires the priest to walk closely with the penitent, offering continuous guidance and support.

In cases involving the so-called "unforgivable sins," the priest's role assumes an additional layer of complexity. He must elucidate the nature of these sins while providing hope for God's infinite mercy. This involves not just theological explanation but a pastoral approach that reassures the penitent of the possibility of forgiveness through sincere repentance. The priest's deep understanding of doctrines and his compassionate ministry are crucial in these delicate situations.

The sacrament of confession is also a testament to the priest's own commitment to his spiritual life. To effectively administer the sacrament, the priest must himself be a man of prayer and penitence, regularly participating in the sacrament of confession. His personal integrity and holiness lend credibility to his ministry and inspire confidence among the faithful. The priest's example of regular confession demonstrates the importance of ongoing spiritual renewal and humility before God.

Ultimately, the priest in the sacrament of confession embodies Christ's healing presence. He stands as an instrument through which the divine mercy flows, transforming souls and restoring them to grace. This sacred duty, steeped in tradition and theology, is a profound manifestation of the Church's mission to bring reconciliation and salvation to humanity.

In conclusion, the role of the priest in the sacrament of confession is multifaceted, demanding a combination of spiritual, pastoral, and theological acumen. He must act as a judge, a healer, a teacher, and a shepherd, guiding the penitent through the process of repentance and reconciliation. This sacred responsibility underscores the priest's indispensable role in the life of the Church and the spiritual well-being of the faithful.

The Penitent's Journey

The journey of the penitent in the Sacrament of Confession is an odyssey marked by inner turmoil, self-reckoning, and hope for divine forgiveness. This chapter delves into that intricate process, dissecting the layers of human emotion and spiritual transformation inherent in seeking absolution for one's sins. As the believer kneels before the confessional, they confront not just the priest cloaked in clerical garb but also the sanctity of the Church and, by extension, the judgment of God.

The essence of this journey is rooted in the recognition of sin. One does not embark on this path lightly; it is a conscious decision born from an acute moral awareness. Cue the moment of realization—a flash of divine illumination that exposes the nature of one's wrongdoing. In Catholic teaching, this is the critical point where the journey truly begins. It's not just about tallying misdemeanors but understanding how one's actions have diverged from the path of righteousness as outlined by Church doctrine. These first steps involve a sincere acknowledgment of having transgressed, setting the stage for genuine repentance.

There is a layered complexity in the penitent's process of self-examination. This involves an introspective inquiry driven by authentic remorse. The penitent is prompted to scrutinize their conscience, peeling back the layers of ego and self-deception. In this grueling examination, one confronts the multifaceted dimensions of sin—sins of commission and omission. Every whisper of moral failure must be exposed to the light.

The notion of contrition occupies a pivotal place in this spiritual journey. Contrition is not merely feeling sorry but experiencing profound sorrow for having offended God. Imperfect contrition, or attrition, arises from a fear of damnation and eternal punishment, juxtaposed with perfect contrition, which flows from a profound love for God and sorrow for having betrayed His divine love. In practice, many penitents grapple with balancing these internal motives, understanding that the depths of their contrition can influence the efficacy of the sacrament.

As one advances along this penitential path, they approach the rites of confession. Here, intimate confessions meet the moral rigor of the priest's guidance. Within the confines of the confessional, the priest represents Christ himself, administering sanctifying grace through absolution. The penitent discloses their sins aloud, each word laden with the weight of spiritual consequence. This verbalization serves a dual purpose: it is both cathartic and juridical, aligning the penitent with the pathways of ecclesiastical discipline.

The role of the priest, in this communicative act, becomes dualistic —both judge and physician. With pastoral sensitivity, the priest listens, assesses, and advises. The ritualistic nature of this sacrament imbues it with an air of solemnity and gravitas. Enigmatic yet paternal, the priest dispenses not mere advice but theological absolution, grounded in divine authority. His role is never mechanical; it demands spiritual sagacity and empathy.

This rite culminates in the act of penance. Penance, or satisfaction, serves as a corrective path, a means to redress the balance upset by sin. It often involves tangible acts—prayers, almsgiving, or other expressions of penitent resolve. However, its true essence lies in fostering moral reformation. Every penance, designed to align the penitent closer to God's will, emphasizes the transformative potential inherent in repentance.

Steeped in both tradition and theology, the journey also necessitates a return path. Post-confession, the penitent reenters the mortal world, yet not as they were before. For true reconciliation, the individual must endeavor to amend their life, seeking to avoid occasions of sin. This continued spiritual vigilance safeguards the grace received and helps maintain a state of sanctifying grace.

Overarching this deeply personal journey is a broader communal significance. The penitent's reconciliation finds its place within the communal body of the Church. Each act of individual absolution contributes to the collective sanctity of the ecclesial community, underscoring the interconnected nature of sin and grace. Therefore, confession is not merely a private matter; it has ecclesiastical and cosmic dimensions. Through the act of contrition and reconciliation, the penitent aligns themselves not only with divine mercy but also with the moral integrity of the Church itself.

In conclusion, the penitent's journey is a tapestry woven with threads of remorse, confession, and penance. It is a pilgrimage through the intricate landscapes of human fallibility and divine grace, a transformative endeavor that echoes the profound theological principles laid out by the Church. It's a testament to the enduring belief in the power of divine forgiveness and the potential for human redemption.

Chapter 5: Forgiveness and Absolution

In the intricate dance of forgiveness and absolution, the Catholic Church's doctrine outlines both a rigorous and compassionate path for the penitent. The conditions for absolution are crystal clear, yet deeply profound: genuine contrition, the confession of all mortal sins, and a firm purpose of amendment. These elements, though seemingly straightforward, carry a weight that can transform the soul. The process of receiving forgiveness is an intimate encounter, facilitating not just the erasure of sins but a rebirth in grace. As the priest pronounces absolution, he acts not merely as a mediator but as a conduit of Divine mercy, rendering the confessional a sacred space where Heaven's justice and compassion converge. This sacramental act is not a mere formality; it is loaded with theological significance, embodying centuries of doctrine that have shaped the complexities and beauties of Catholic confession.

Conditions for Absolution

The Catholic Church's doctrines on absolution weave a complex tapestry of theological and canonical stipulations. To grasp the profound soul-healing grace that comes with absolution, one must understand the meticulous standards set forth by the Church. For absolution to be granted, several critical conditions must be met, which form an intricate dance between divine justice and mercy.

At the forefront of these conditions is contrition, a genuine sorrow for one's sins. But not just any sorrow will do; it must be sincere and heartfelt. The Church delineates between perfect and imperfect contrition. Perfect contrition arises from a love for God above all else, while imperfect contrition stems from a recognition of sin's ugliness or fear of eternal damnation. Although perfect contrition is ideal, the Church, in its wisdom, accepts imperfect contrition within the sacrament as sufficient for absolution, provided it includes a firm resolve to sin no more.

Equally pivotal is the verbal confession of sins to a priest. This requirement, rooted in the ancient practices of the Church, underscores the dual dimensions of sin: personal and communal. By confessing to a priest, who embodies the Church and acts in persona Christi, the penitent acknowledges not only their personal failings but also the rupture they have caused within the larger ecclesial body. Thus, the act of confession is twofold, mending both the individual's relationship with God and their bond with the Church community.

Of course, confession must be complete. This means the penitent must strive to recall and confess all mortal sins since their last confession. Deliberate concealment of any grave sin jeopardizes the validity of the absolution received, underscoring the necessity for transparency and integrity during the sacramental encounter. The Church doesn't demand perfect memory but insists on honest effort.

After confessing sins, the penitent receives a penance, an outward act that symbolizes inner transformation. Penance serves multiple purposes. It is both an expression of the penitent's sorrow and a tangible means of reparation. Furthermore, it acts as a catalyst for spiritual growth, helping the individual detach from sinful habits and align more closely with God's will. The Church views penance not as a punitive measure but as a therapeutic one—an antidote to the poison of sin.

Integral to the process is the intent to reform one's life. Merely confessing sins without a genuine intention to avoid future sin renders the sacrament hollow. The Church sees this resolve as a binding promise to pursue holiness, relying on God's grace to avoid occasions of sin and to cultivate virtue. This intent is closely scrutinized by the confessor, whose role includes discerning the penitent's earnestness and providing appropriate spiritual guidance.

The backdrop to these conditions is the role of the priest, who acts not just as a passive listener, but as a spiritual physician. With the authority bestowed upon him by the Church, the priest offers absolution, freeing the penitent from the burden of sin. This absolution is not merely a formality but a powerful act of divine mercy, transforming the penitent's soul through God's grace. The priest's discernment and pastoral care are crucial in guiding the penitent through the sacrament, ensuring that all conditions for absolution are met.

It is worth noting the doctrinal rigor underpinning these practices. The Church, through centuries of theological development, has meticulously articulated these conditions to preserve the sacrament's integrity. Canon law, a corpus of ecclesiastical regulations, codifies these requirements to ensure uniformity and faithfulness to apostolic tradition. Thus, adherence to these conditions is not merely a matter of personal piety but one of ecclesial obedience and unity.

Moreover, these conditions, while stringent, reflect the Church's understanding of human frailty and divine mercy. The sacrament of confession acknowledges the reality of human imperfection and offers a divine remedy, finely balancing justice and mercy. By mandating honest confession, sincere contrition, and a firm purpose of amendment, the Church ensures that the penitent's approach to the sacrament is genuine and transformative.

The implications of these conditions extend beyond individual forgiveness. They underscore a theology that sees sin as not just a personal offense but a communal disruption. Absolution, therefore, is an act of ecclesial healing, reinstating the penitent within the Body of Christ. This communal dimension is vital, reminding the faithful that their actions impact the wider Church, and their reconciliation restores harmony within the ecclesial community.

In conclusion, the conditions for absolution within the Catholic Church are a testament to its profound understanding of sin, repentance, and divine grace. They are designed to ensure that the sacrament of confession remains a genuine encounter with God's mercy, fostering true spiritual renewal. By adhering to these conditions, the faithful are not only reconciled with God but are also reintegrated into the life of the Church, embodying the unity and sanctity to which all are called.

The Process of Receiving Forgiveness

The process of receiving forgiveness within the Catholic Church is a journey marked by the soul's earnest striving for reconciliation with God. Such a process is deeply rooted in the Church's sacramental theology, particularly within the Sacrament of Confession. As moral theologians, canon lawyers, and devout Roman Catholics ponder the gravity of sin and the holiness of absolution, it is essential that we dissect this process with both nuance and devotion.

First and foremost, the act of contrition represents the initial stirring of the heart towards penance. The penitent must acknowledge their sinfulness and feel genuine remorse. This remorse might be derived from a love for God (perfect contrition) or from a fear of eternal damnation (imperfect contrition). Both forms must be sincerely confessed within the Sacrament of Confession to be efficacious, yet the Church teaches that even imperfect contrition can suffice when coupled with the sacrament.

Upon entering the confessional, the penitent kneels, aware of their humility before God and the priest, who serves as the mediator. This act not only underscores the recognition of one's sins but also a submission to the Church's authority. The confessional space itself, silent and often dimly lit, evokes a sense of solemnity and deep reflection, an environment designed to facilitate the soul's introspection and the heart's penitence.

The confession itself is more than a recitation of errors; it is a profound encounter with divine mercy. As the penitent speaks, there is an unburdening of the soul. Each sin is a thread removed, each word a step closer to spiritual liberty. The priest listens with both empathy and authority, aware that he is entrusted with the keys to the Kingdom, as Christ imparted to Saint Peter. He is to offer spiritual guidance, prescribe penance, and ultimately, grant absolution.

Penance is the tangible action that follows the confession of sins. Its role cannot be understated. Varied in form, from prayers to good deeds, penance acts as a means to repair the spiritual damage wrought by sin. The penitent, in fulfilling these acts, aligns themselves with the path of righteousness once more. It is a bridge between the remorse felt and the forgiveness offered, connecting intention to action.

The words of absolution spoken by the priest are not mere formalities; they are believed to be transformative. "I absolve you from your sins," he declares, invoking the power vested in him by Christ himself. This moment crystallizes the entire process—the weight of sin lifted and the grace of God flooding the penitent's soul. Herein lies the beauty of Catholic absolution; it personifies the divine mercy that is both freely given and yet, through the acts of contrition and penance, diligently sought.

The cyclical nature of sin and absolution highlights the Christian journey. While absolution cleanses the soul, the vigilance against future sin must bolster the penitent. It is a reminder of the human condition —prone to sin but also capable of divine grace. Therefore, the process of receiving forgiveness does not end with absolution; it extends into the living of a renewed life, one that strives to avoid occasions of sin and seeks continual spiritual growth.

Understanding canonical perspectives aids in comprehending the comprehensive nature of this process. The Church's canon law provides stringent guidelines to ensure the sacrament's integrity and efficacy. For instance, Canons 959-963 outline the requisites for receiving this sacrament validly. The penitent must have at least imperfect contrition, a genuine purpose of amendment, and a confession of all mortal sins.

Moreover, the history of the Sacrament of Confession has evolved to reach its present form, balancing justice and mercy. Early Christians practiced public penance, an arduous expression of contrition, yet through time, the Church recognized the need for privacy in confession, hence the personal confessional. This transformation underscores the Church's adaptability and enduring commitment to fostering genuine repentance within the hearts of believers.

It is worth acknowledging the tension that exists between the theological constructs of 'unforgivable sins' and the principles underpinning the forgiveness offered through confession. This tension challenges theologians to delve deeper into the mysterious interplay of divine justice and mercy. While the Church, influenced by scriptural interpretations and theological debate, maintains certain sins as particularly grave, it also upholds the boundless nature of God's merciful love.

In conclusion, the process of receiving forgiveness in the Catholic tradition unfolds as a potent interplay between human acknowledgment of sin and the divine offer of grace. Each element, from contrition to penance and absolution, weaves together to form a holistic pathway to spiritual renewal. For moral theologians, Roman Catholics, and canon lawyers, unpacking these layers is not merely an academic endeavor but a pilgrimage into the heart of divine mercy and justice. Thus, the sacramental journey toward forgiveness is both a personal and communal testament to the enduring promise of salvation through Christ.

Chapter 6: The Ã¢Â€ÂœUnforgivable SinÃ¢Â€Â⬧

The notion of the "unforgivable sin" has long tormented the hearts of the faithful, evoking images of eternal condemnation that even the sacrament of confession cannot cure. Rooted in the Gospels, particularly in the words attributed to Jesus about blasphemy against the Holy Spirit, this concept transcends mere doctrinal debate, seeping into the spiritual marrow of Roman Catholic ethics. The theological labyrinth surrounding this sin finds a vivid interlocutor in Saint Alphonsus Liguori's writings, where he contends with its implications vis-à-vis God's boundless mercy and justice. Scholars and faithful alike have grappled with reconciling the idea of an unforgivable act with the Church's teachings on contrition and absolution. The debate intensifies when considering imperfect contrition—sorrow for sin stirred more by fear of damnation than by love of God—raising profound questions about the nature of true repentance. As we navigate these treacherous theological waters, it becomes evident that the tension between divine mercy and justice is not merely a matter of doctrinal exactitude, but a profound mystery echoing the complexity of the human soul in its quest for redemption.

The "Unforgivable Sin"
Scriptural Basis

The concept of the "unforgivable sin" has its roots deeply embedded in Scripture. To understand this notion, one must first turn to the texts that elucidate it most clearly, particularly the Gospels of the New Testament. One of the primary passages addressing the "unforgivable sin" is found in the Gospel of Matthew. Jesus declares, "And so I tell you, every kind of sin and slander can be forgiven, but blasphemy against the Spirit will not be forgiven" (Matthew 12:31, NIV). This stark pronouncement immediately begs the question: Why is blasphemy against the Holy Spirit deemed unforgivable?

The context of this statement is integral. Jesus makes this proclamation after performing a miracle, healing a demon-possessed man who was both blind and mute. The Pharisees, witnessing this, accuse Jesus of casting out demons by the power of Beelzebul, the prince of demons. Jesus rebukes them, indicating that such a belief—that His holy work comes from an unholy source—constitutes a profound misalignment with the truth. Essentially, Jesus identifies their blatant rejection of the Holy Spirit's evident work as blasphemy, rendering this sin unforgivable because it encapsulates a complete and deliberate turning away from God's truth.

Luke's Gospel also weighs in on the matter, with a similar passage: "And everyone who speaks a word against the Son of Man will be forgiven, but anyone who blasphemes against the Holy Spirit will not be forgiven" (Luke 12:10, NIV). This repetition emphasizes the gravity and consistency of Jesus' message across different traditions within the early Christian community. Concomitantly, Mark's parallel account in his Gospel further solidifies the narrative, thereby highlighting its importance within the New Testament corpus.

The Apostle Paul, in his epistle to the Hebrews, provides additional layers of understanding. He writes, "If we deliberately keep on sinning after we have received the knowledge of the truth, no sacrifice for sins is left, but only a fearful expectation of judgment" (Hebrews 10:26-27, NIV). This passage isn't explicitly about blasphemy against the Holy Spirit, yet it underscores a similar principle: a willful and persistent rejection of God's salvific work leaves one bereft of recourse.

Church Fathers, including St. Augustine and St. Thomas Aquinas, grappled with these passages. Augustine interprets the unforgivable sin as a state of obstinacy: a heart so hardened that it continually resists grace. Aquinas further clarifies, suggesting that blasphemy against the

Holy Spirit represents a final impenitence—a complete refusal to repent and accept God's mercy. This lies in stark contrast to mere human weakness or error; it is a deliberate and persistent rejection of grace, an active and perpetual denial of the truth.

The Catechism of the Catholic Church integrates these scriptural and theological insights, defining blasphemy against the Holy Spirit as a sin "that includes the deliberate refusal to accept God's mercy by repenting, rejecting the salvation God offers to man through the Holy Spirit" (CCC 1864). Thus, the unforgivable sin stands as a conscious and ultimate rejection of the Spirit's sanctifying power.

In probing these scriptural passages, it becomes clear that the unforgivable sin isn't an arbitrary or isolated concept. It is woven into the broader fabric of Christian soteriology and ecclesiology. By rejecting the Holy Spirit's intrinsic role in the life of believers, one severs the lifeline to forgiveness. In essence, it is not that God withholds forgiveness, but rather that the sinner places themselves beyond its reach by rejecting the very means through which grace is dispensed.

An essential factor to consider is the intended audience of these scriptural admonitions. Jesus' warnings to the Pharisees and teachings to His disciples highlight the universal need for humility and openness to God's grace. The Pharisees' tragic flaw lies in their spiritual pride and refusal to acknowledge the divine origin of Jesus' works, thereby exemplifying the unforgivable sin. Modern Catholic thought encourages believers to reflect on these passages, not as a source of fear, but as a call to remain vigilant against spiritual complacency and pride.

Moreover, the scriptural basis for the unforgivable sin invites a deeper exploration of the relationship between human freedom and divine mercy. Paul's teachings, particularly those in Romans, emphasize that while grace abounds, it must be received. "Where sin increased, grace increased all the more" (Romans 5:20, NIV), yet this grace does not compel; it invites. The refusal of this invitation, especially one so profound as the Holy Spirit's indwelling presence, constitutes the very crux of the unforgivable sin.

To illustrate, consider Jesus' parable of the prodigal son. While the son's initial departure and subsequent return are pivotal, imagine if he had stubbornly refused to acknowledge his father upon his return. The father's love remained constant, but the son's reception of that love required humility and repentance. This dynamic is mirrored in the scriptural discussion of the unforgivable sin: God's mercy is ever-present, but its transformative power depends on human acquiescence.

Hence, theologians, canonists, and moral philosophers must meticulously study these scriptural texts within their proper contexts. This involves not only exegetical precision but also a comprehensive understanding of the historical and cultural milieu in which these teachings were given. The unforgivable sin is not a capricious edict but a fundamental aspect of humanity's relational dynamic with the divine.

In conclusion, the scriptural basis for the "unforgivable sin" offers a profound meditation on the interplay between divine grace and human freedom. It underscores the necessity of openness to the Holy Spirit's sanctifying work, warning against the perils of spiritual pride and obstinacy. As moral theologians, Roman Catholics, and canon lawyers, engaging with these sacred texts calls for a nuanced and empathetic approach, one which recognizes the boundless potential of God's mercy and the tragic possibility of its rejection.

Liguori's Perspective

As we venture into the intricate realm of "The Unforgivable Sin," Alphonsus Liguori's religious scholarship provides a uniquely compelling perspective. The essence of Liguori's theology emphasizes both the gravity of such a sin and the boundless potential for divine forgiveness—a paradox that demands probing insight. His nuanced comprehension of sin, particularly the notion of the unforgivable, is an culminating contribution to Catholic moral theology.

Liguori meticulously dissected the nature of sin through the lens of mercy and justice, weaving them into the fabric of his theological framework. He argued that while many sins merit grave concern, the so-called "unforgivable sin" isn't easily transgressed. For Liguori, blasphemy against the Holy Spirit—a deliberate, entrenched refusal to accept God's mercy and forgiveness—represents the pinnacle of human rebellion. It is not merely a casual act of defiance, but a profound rejection that renders repentance almost impossible.

Yet, Liguori's teachings do not portray an unfeeling God quick to condemn. Instead, he illustrates a deity perpetually yearning for repentance and reconciliation. He believed that understanding the context and the condition of one's heart is crucial when considering the nature of their sin, even when it seems unforgivable. For Liguori, the unforgivable sin is not a moment of weakness or doubt; it is a persistent, obstinate refusal to be touched by God's grace.

Interestingly, Liguori's approach intertwines with the broader theological discourse on the limits of free will versus divine mercy. He endorsed Augustine's perspective that human beings possess free will, yet they can't achieve true repentance without divine aid. Consequently, he perceived the unforgivable sin as a deliberate rejection of this divine assistance.

In his writings, Liguori employs a tone reminiscent of a moral detective, patiently unraveling the complexities of the human soul. He emphasized that while God's mercy is boundless, it is not extended without discerning the authenticity of contrition. For him, a heart that remains impenetrable to God's love and forgiveness essentially bars itself from redemption, and thus from absolution.

Moreover, Liguori highlighted the role of education and pastoral guidance in preventing the descent into the unforgivable sin. He firmly believed in confession as a means of enlightenment and moral rectitude, wherein both the penitent and the priest play significant roles. This reciprocal engagement aims to soften hearts and open them to divine mercy, making the notion of an unforgivable sin increasingly rare.

While delving deeply into Liguori's treatises, one notices his persistence in underscoring the spiritual journey of the individual. His theological narratives envision contrition as a moment of profound self-reckoning. He vividly describes the horrors that accompany unrepentant sin, yet consistently returns to a vision of hope rooted in God's merciful nature.

Liguori also engaged with contemporary theological debates on the ultimate fate of individuals who might commit the unforgivable sin. His contributions provide a distinct balance amidst various theological opinions, arguing neither for a lenient dismissal of the gravity of sin nor for an inveterate condemnation devoid of compassion. Instead, he champions a robust interplay between justice and mercy, upholding the Catholic tenet that no soul is beyond the reach of divine love, barring their own obstinate defiance.

Ultimately, Liguori's thoughts on the unforgivable sin draw from an intricate blend of doctrinal fidelity and pastoral sensitivity. His perspective underscores the persistent call for repentance and the celebration of divine mercy, underpinning the sacramental act of confession with profound theological depth. His insights continue to offer moral theologians, Roman Catholics, and Canon lawyers a rich tapestry of wisdom, balancing fear of eternal separation with the perennial hope of redemption.

Theological Debate

The concept of the "unforgivable sin," often attributed to blasphemy against the Holy Spirit, generates significant theological debate within the Catholic tradition. This debate is not merely academic but impacts pastoral care and the sacramental life of the Church. The implications of deeming a sin unforgivable challenge the core tenets of mercy, contrition, and redemption that guide Catholic teaching.

In the Gospels, particularly in Mark 3:28-30 and Matthew 12:31-32, Christ warns of a sin that "will not be forgiven." Scholars, theologians, and clergy have long wrestled with these passages, seeking to understand and articulate their meanings. Theologians such as Saint Augustine and Thomas Aquinas grappled with these texts, endeavoring to balance divine justice with God's infinite mercy.

Saint Alphonsus Liguori contributed significantly to this discourse. His theological framework emphasizes the importance of contrition and the conditions necessary for absolution. Liguori posits that while God's mercy is boundless, it necessitates genuine repentance from the sinner, and herein lies part of the complexity. If a sinner refuses to acknowledge their transgressions or remains obstinate in their sin, how can mercy be applied?

One central issue in these debates is the nature of the unforgivable sin itself. Is this sin a specific act, or is it a state of being? Many theologians argue that the unforgivable sin encompasses a persistent state of unrepentance and a conscious, deliberate rejection of God's grace. This interpretation asserts that it is not merely the blasphemous act that is unforgivable but the hardened heart that refuses God's mercy.

Theological perspectives vary on this issue. Some argue that the unforgivable sin is a rare and extreme condition, while others maintain that it might be a more pressing pastoral concern. The Second Vatican Council, in its approach to modernizing and contextualizing Church doctrine, refrained from giving a definitive position on this matter, leaving room for ongoing interpretation and discussion.

Moreover, the role of imperfect contrition in the context of the unforgivable sin presents another layer of complexity. Imperfect contrition, often driven by a fear of divine punishment rather than pure love for God, is still regarded as a valid form of repentance within moral theology. The question emerges: Can someone experiencing only imperfect contrition be guilty of the unforgivable sin if they subsequently strive for a fuller conversion?

With imperfect contrition, the Church acknowledges human frailty and the journey towards spiritual maturity. It recognizes that fear of God's punishment can catalyze genuine repentance, opening the door to divine grace. This view aligns with Liguori's thoughts, which stress

God's readiness to accept any form of sincere repentance, even if it begins with fear.

However, opponents of this inclusive interpretation argue that the unforgivable sin must logically exist as a counterbalance to the notion of complete forgiveness and mercy. They claim that without it, the concept of sin loses its weight and seriousness. There is a need for an absolute limit—one that underscores the gravity of obstinate sinfulness and the deliberate refusal of God's salvific grace.

On the other hand, some theologians argue for a more radical understanding of God's mercy. Following this line of reasoning, God's grace is ultimately irresistible and transformative. According to this perspective, any person clinging to sin may someday encounter an overwhelming grace that softens their heart and leads them to repentance. The unforgivable sin, in this context, is seen less as an actual barrier but as a metaphorical representation of the ultimate seriousness of rejecting grace.

This theological debate extends to practical pastoral applications. Priests and confessors often find themselves at the intersection of doctrine and individual conscience. If a penitent expresses fear of having committed the unforgivable sin, the confessor must navigate the fine line between offering hope and maintaining the gravity of persistent, unrepentant sin.

One noteworthy area of this debate involves the balance between warning against the severity of sin and discouraging despair. Overemphasis on the unforgivable sin can lead to spiritual despair, where individuals believe they are beyond redemption. Conversely, an overemphasis on mercy without acknowledging the seriousness of sin undermines the call to genuine repentance and the transformative power of grace.

Canon lawyers and moral theologians have attempted to delineate specific guidelines around these questions, but the inherent ambiguity of the topic ensures that no singular answer suffices. The Catechism of the Catholic Church provides some clarity but leaves ample room for interpretation, reflecting the dynamic and evolving nature of this theological inquiry.

Ultimately, the debate over the unforgivable sin functions as a microcosm of broader theological tensions within the Church. It encapsulates the struggle to balance justice and mercy, divine omnipotence and human free will, and the immediate pastoral needs versus eternal doctrinal truths. All these elements underscore the profound and often mysterious nature of the Catholic faith.

As Catholics continue to reflect on these issues, the role of the theologian, canon lawyer, and moral teacher remains vital. These experts serve not only as interpreters of doctrine but as guides for the faithful, helping them navigate the complexities of sin, repentance, and grace. The debate over the unforgivable sin is not isolated but interconnected with other fundamental aspects of Catholic theology.

Moreover, discussions on this subject often lead back to the centrality of love in the Christian doctrine. Perfect contrition, described as sorrow for sin out of love for God, remains the ideal within the moral framework. By aspiring towards love rather than fear, the faithful engage deeply with the transformative potential of grace.

In conclusion, the unresolved nature of the theological debate over the unforgivable sin invites deeper contemplation and reflection. It challenges both theologians and the lay faithful to engage with the profound mysteries of faith, prompting a continual re-examination of one's relationship with God, contrition, and the power of divine mercy.

Chapter 7: Imperfect Contrition and the Fear of God

The intricate dance between imperfect contrition and the fear of God has long occupied the minds and hearts of theologians. Imperfect contrition, often driven by a fear of divine retribution rather than pure love for God, presents a theological conundrum within the Catholic framework. The soul's struggle between love and fear while approaching repentance shades the sacrament of confession with layers of complexity. Historically, the Church has wrestled with understanding the role that fear should play in the process of returning to God's grace. Should fear merely be a preliminary step, motivating the sinner toward perfect contrition? Or does it possess salvific value in its own right? Unraveling this dilemma requires a deep dive into ecclesiastical teachings, the writings of saints, and the lived experiences of the faithful, exposing the tension that pervades the path to spiritual reconciliation. Embracing imperfect contrition without dismissing the reverential fear it entails offers a nuanced appreciation of humanity's arduous journey to divine absolution.

Understanding Imperfect Contrition

In the realm of moral theology, the concept of contrition distinguishes itself through its nuanced layers. Imperfect contrition, otherwise known as attrition, stands particularly intriguing due to its inherent complexity and profound implications. Unlike perfect contrition, which stems from the pure love of God above all else, imperfect contrition finds its roots in a more self-centered motivation—the fear of eternal punishment or the ugliness of sin's consequences.

Historically, the Catholic Church has grappled with understanding and categorizing the different motivations behind human repentance. While perfect contrition is ideal, being driven by the love for God, imperfect contrition has also been granted a prominent place in the Church's teachings, sacraments, and pastoral practices. Imperfect contrition can still lead to forgiveness when it culminates in the sacrament of confession. This makes it a topic worthy of deep examination.

To grasp the essence of imperfect contrition, one must start by examining the different emotions and rationales that prompt a sinner to seek reconciliation with God. Imperfect contrition often arises from the fear of Hell, the dread of God's just retribution, or the realization of the moral and spiritual degradation that sin causes. This type of contrition is characterized by a recognition of guilt and the awareness of offending divine justice, yet it lacks the complete detachment from sin that perfect love for God inspires.

Even within its imperfections, this type of contrition holds immense value in the economy of salvation. Its acceptance by the Church underscores the infinite mercy of God and His desire for the sinner's return to grace, regardless of the initial motives. As long as the contrition is genuine and the sinner's intention is to confess and amend their life, imperfect contrition suffices to receive absolution in the sacrament of confession.

Saint Alphonsus Liguori, one of the key theological minds to delve deeply into this concept, postulated that while perfect contrition is superior and more desirable, imperfect contrition is still an essential stepping stone towards full repentance. His works highlight that the fear of God, which leads to imperfect contrition, can be instrumental in guiding the sinner back to the path of righteousness.

The dynamic tension between perfect and imperfect contrition not only sheds light on human frailty but also magnifies the boundless grace offered through the sacraments. The sacrament of confession, or reconciliation, is where this interplay most vividly comes to life. The penitent, driven perhaps more by fear than love, still finds God's mercy waiting. They arrive with a heart not yet fully aligned with divine love but deeply yearning for restoration and forgiveness.

It's essential to question and reflect on the role fear plays in the context of contrition. While contemporary theology often aims to emphasize a loving relationship with God, the ancient notion of the fear of the Lord retains a significant, albeit complex, place in Catholic teaching. Proverbs 1:7 proclaims that "The fear of the Lord is the beginning of knowledge," suggesting that this fear can indeed lead to true wisdom and subsequently deeper love.

Some argue that in modern pastoral care, there's an undue focus on portraying God solely through the lens of love and mercy, potentially neglecting the wholesome fear that engenders genuine contrition.

Moral theologians often debate whether stressing God's justice more could cultivate a more authentic repentance among the faithful. Given human nature's tendency towards complacency, the fear associated with imperfect contrition may act as a necessary catalyst for a genuine transformation of heart.

Moreover, it's worth noting that imperfect contrition does not undermine the gravity of sin; rather, it approaches sin's seriousness from a different angle. For instance, a sinner who fears Hell recognizes the gravity of offending God and the cosmic order, even if this recognition springs from self-preservation rather than pure love. This fear can serve as the groundwork for a deeper, more perfect contrition as the penitent grows in spiritual maturity and love for God.

The Catholic Church, through its doctrines and the sacrament of penance, provides a structure that honors both forms of contrition. This structure supports the spiritual journey from fear to love, a path trodden by countless saints and sinners alike. Pope John Paul II eloquently stated in *Reconciliatio et Paenitentia* about the profound nature of reconciliation that begins with recognizing one's sinfulness and the fear of God's just wrath.

The sacrament itself stands as a testimony to God's willingness to accept even the most imperfect repentance, providing that the penitent earnestly seeks His mercy. Through confession, absolution, and the subsequent acts of penance, the Church nurtures the penitent's growth towards perfect contrition. Thus, imperfect contrition must not be seen as a lower form of repentance but rather as an initial yet important stage in the journey towards full reconciliation with God.

This understanding necessitates a compassionate pastoral approach. Confessors, aware of human fragility, guide penitents with patience, helping them transition from fear-based repentance to one inspired by love. This dual acknowledgment of fear and love in contrition exemplifies the Church's holistic understanding of human nature and divine mercy.

It must also be recognized that imperfect contrition, interestingly, opens up a dialogue between fear and love in the heart of the Church itself. The Church, modeled after Christ's own ministry, always balances justice with mercy, ensuring that the sinner's return is both encouraged and celebrated. The sacrament of confession becomes the arena where imperfect contrition meets divine forgiveness, transforming it into an opportunity for spiritual growth and deeper connection with God.

In today's theological landscape, discussions surrounding imperfect contrition and the fear of God remain as relevant as ever. They server as a reminder that while human motivations may start impurely, the journey towards God is full of opportunities for purification and sanctification. The history and evolution of these theological insights reflect the Church's ongoing dedication to understanding the human condition in all its complexity, and its unyielding commitment to leading souls towards salvation.

Thus, understanding imperfect contrition demands a balance of theological insight and pastoral sensitivity. It requires recognizing the full spectrum of human emotion and motivation while continuously pointing towards the ultimate goal—union with God through sincere repentance and conversion. This dynamic tension between imperfection and grace ultimately reveals the profound depths of God's mercy and the Church's mission to bring every soul back to Him, however falteringly the journey may begin.

Fear vs. Love in Repentance

Within the realm of moral theology, the tension between fear and love in repentance is a subject of considerable depth and nuance. Imperfect contrition, characterized by sorrow for sin arising from the fear of eternal damnation, stands in stark contrast to perfect contrition, which is born out of love for God above all else. The distinction, though subtle, has profound implications for the sacrament of confession and the forgiveness of sins.

In Catholic theology, the concept of imperfect contrition acknowledges human fragility and the innate tendency towards self-preservation. When an individual repents out of fear of God's just punishment, this fear is not merely an emotional response but a recognition of God's righteous authority. The Church teaches that even this imperfect form of repentance, when accompanied by the sacrament of confession, suffices for absolution.

The central question here is why fear, rather than love, can lead to true repentance. The answer lies in the nature of what it means to be human. Fear of divine retribution awakens the conscience to the gravity of sin. It's a primal response, ingrained in our survival instincts. The presence of fear signals an awareness of God's omnipotence and justice, which in turn can initiate the journey towards a deeper relationship with God—a relationship that ideally progresses towards love.

However, critics argue that repentance motivated by fear alone might reflect a utilitarian mindset, concerned more with avoiding punishment than with genuine conversion of heart. This criticism isn't without merit. Moral theologians have long debated the validity of such repentance and whether it truly meets the criteria for a turning away from sin. Despite these debates, Church doctrine remains clear: while imperfect contrition lacks the purity of perfect contrition, it is a starting point that opens the door to God's grace.

St. Alphonsus Liguori, a towering figure in moral theology, delved deeply into this dichotomy. He emphasized that while perfect contrition is the ideal, the Church must recognize human limitations. According to Liguori, God's mercy is vast and compassionate, extending even to those whose repentance is imperfect. This theological stance ensures that salvation remains accessible to all, not just to those who achieve the lofty goal of perfect contrition.

Further, in pastoral practice, priests are often tasked with guiding penitents who grapple with imperfect contrition. The confessional becomes a space where fear of God's judgment is acknowledged but gradually transformed into genuine love and contrition. The priest's role is to nurture this transformation, offering not just absolution but also spiritual guidance aimed at deepening the penitent's relationship with God.

To understand the dynamic between fear and love in repentance, it's essential to also consider the scriptural foundation. The Bible abundantly references both fear of the Lord and love for Him as fundamental to faith. Proverbs 1:7 states, "The fear of the Lord is the beginning of knowledge," while 1 John 4:18 asserts, "There is no fear in love; but perfect love casts out fear." This apparent dichotomy isn't a contradiction but rather an invitation to a holistic understanding of the divine-human relationship.

Penitents often find themselves at the intersection of fear and love, teetering between a dread of divine wrath and a desire to return to God. The two emotions are not mutually exclusive but can be seen as part of a continuum in the spiritual journey. Fear, though initially dominant, can evolve into a more profound love and perfect contrition as the penitent grows in faith.

The historical development of the Church's teaching on contrition has also reflected this balance. Medieval theologians like Thomas Aquinas have maintained that imperfect contrition, while necessary, should lead the sinner towards perfect contrition. In this way, the fear of God acts as a preparatory step, paving the way for a more complete sense of repentance grounded in love.

The interplay between fear and love can be likened to the stages of spiritual maturation. Just as a child initially obeys parents out of fear of punishment but grows to understand and love them, so too can a sinner begin with fear and move towards a loving, contrite heart. The sacrament of confession serves as the pivotal juncture where this transformation is both symbolized and actualized.

Therefore, the role of fear in repentance should not be dismissed lightly. It's a necessary component of the journey towards salvation, sanctioned by centuries of theological discourse and pastoral practice. The Church, in its wisdom, accommodates this aspect of human experience, urging believers to strive for perfect contrition but comforting them with the assurance of God's mercy even in their imperfection.

In sum, the tension between fear and love in repentance encapsulates the human condition's complexity. It is a journey marked by struggle, growth, and divine grace. As moral theologians, canon lawyers, and Roman Catholics reflect upon this dynamic, they contribute to a richer understanding of the sacrament of confession and its integral role in the Christian life. By embracing both fear and love, the faithful can approach the throne of grace with humility, trusting in God's boundless compassion.

Chapter 8: Moral TheologyÃ¢Â€Â™s Toughest Questions

In this labyrinth of moral theology, the quandaries surrounding true repentance and the notion of unforgivable sins cast long shadows over the doctrines that have guided Roman Catholics for centuries. The debate rages on—what constitutes an authentic act of contrition? Does imperfect contrition tainted by fear hold any weight compared to the profound sorrow driven by love for God? The dilemma deepens when considering the so-called 'unforgivable sins.' Are there truly transgressions so dire that they forever sever the thread between the sinner and divine grace? The history of confession, heavily imbued with these theological conundrums, reflects the Catholic Church's evolving understanding as it seeks to balance justice with mercy. We unravel these challenging questions, probing the very core of human fallibility and divine forgiveness, echoing the persistent struggle to align mortal imperfections with heavenly expectations.

What Constitutes True Repentance?

What does it mean to truly repent? This question sits at the heart of moral theology, challenging even the most seasoned theologians,

Roman Catholics, and Canon lawyers. It bears implications not merely for theoretical discourse but delves into the practical spirituality outlined in the Sacrament of Confession. In wrestling with true repentance, we are called to balance profound sorrow for sin with an equally strong intention to amend one's life. Yet, it is here that the waters become murky, straddling the line between the perfect state of contrition and the more commonplace imperfect contrition.

Catholic teaching makes a clear distinction between perfect and imperfect contrition. Perfect contrition arises from a love of God above all else, whereas imperfect contrition, often referred to as attrition, is primarily motivated by fear of divine punishment. Undoubtedly, perfect contrition is ideal, and it is this that paves the way for true repentance. However, in the realm of daily human experience, imperfect contrition is far more frequent. Herein lies the tension—can true repentance be rooted in a fear of damnation rather than an unadulterated love of God?

The history of the Church's teachings sheds light on this dilemma. Saint Alphonsus Liguori, a pivotal figure in moral theology, contended that imperfect contrition, when coupled with the Sacrament of Confession, can lead to forgiveness. This understanding provides a lifeline to many believers who struggle to attain the sublime state of perfect contrition. It emphasizes God's readiness to embrace even those who approach Him with less than perfect motives.

Yet, to grasp the full essence of true repentance, one must recognize that it encompasses more than just an emotional or psychological state. Repentance is fundamentally transformative. It calls for a radical reorientation of one's life and values towards God's will. True repentance engenders tangible acts of penance and charity, manifesting an authentic commitment to moral and spiritual conversion.

The Church has long acknowledged the multidimensional nature of repentance. Historically, penance and indulgences played central roles in the expression of true repentance, serving as both external symbols and practical proofs of one's inner contrition. By undertaking acts of penance, believers externalize their commitment to change, reflecting an inner moral and spiritual reformation.

It's essential to explore the scriptural foundations underpinning true repentance to further understand its intricacies. The parable of the Prodigal Son (Luke 15:11-32) poignantly illustrates the elements of true repentance: recognition of one's sins, a heartfelt return to the Father, and a decision to amend one's life. The son's return is marked by both a sincere sorrow for his transgressions and a genuine intention to change—a dual aspect echoing the necessity for both contrition and amendment in true repentance.

However, could there be sins so grievous that they transcend the bounds of forgiveness, even when sincere repentance is present? Here, the discussion intersects with the concept of the "unforgivable sin," which theologians have debated for centuries. Within this theological framework, true repentance takes on an even more significant role, potentially acting as the linchpin that determines one's eternal fate.

Repentance cannot exist in isolation; it requires the sacramental grace available through Confession. The act of confessing one's sins to a priest serves not only as a means of absolution but also as an affirmation of one's intention to pursue a path aligned with divine will. The penitent emerges from the confessional not merely empty-handed but renewed, reinvigorated by the grace of absolution and poised for moral transformation.

Yet, discerning whether one has genuinely achieved true repentance can be elusive. Saint Augustine poignantly remarked that "true repentance is to cease from sin." Thus, a measuring stick for true repentance could be the degree to which one distances oneself from prior sins, both in thought and deed. Yet, given human fallibility, repeated failures often obscured by secular temptations can complicate this self-assessment.

Manuals of moral theology have long provided guidance on examining one's conscience, intending to assist the faithful in discerning the authenticity of their repentance. Such examinations typically delve into both the gravity of the sin and the sincere resolve to avoid future transgressions. The juxtaposition between one's conscience and the Church's teachings often reveals deeper self-awareness, leading to more profound repentance.

Moreover, contrition and repentance touch the core of Christian teaching regarding mercy and forgiveness. Divine mercy offers a path to redemption that transcends human frailty. Even those who approach God with imperfect contrition find themselves wrapped in His boundless love, provided their repentance is genuine, albeit scoped through the lens of their human limitations.

This understanding frames true repentance not as an unachievable ideal but as an attainable, ongoing journey toward spiritual betterment. Realistically, most believers find themselves navigating the tumultuous waters of imperfect contrition, aspiring towards a more perfect love of God that illuminates and guides their repentance. By fostering an environment of continuous self-examination, aided by sacramental grace, the Church encourages the faithful to strive towards true repentance, encapsulating both profound sorrow for sin and a fervent resolve to amend their lives.

Contemporary pastoral theology also offers insights into the evolving understanding of true repentance. In an era marked by complex moral landscapes, what constitutes true repentance demands a nuanced approach. The Church's role morphs into a beacon of guidance, helping believers traverse their spiritual journeys amidst modern-day distractions and moral ambiguities.

In conclusion, true repentance, encompassing both perfect and imperfect contrition, remains an intricate tapestry woven from the threads of sorrow, intention, and divine grace. It is a testament to the dynamic interplay between human effort and divine assistance, inviting the faithful to persistently seek a heart aligned with God's will. Continually evolving yet rooted in timeless truths, true repentance calls us to an ever-deeper embrace of divine love, manifesting in both contrition and a resolute transformation of life.

Are Some Sins Truly Unforgivable?

The question of whether some sins are truly unforgivable has long haunted the corridors of moral theology. It is a perplexing enigma that immerses theologians, priests, and laypeople in a labyrinth of ethical and doctrinal queries. The core of this debate often centers around the nature of contrition and the strength of one's repentance. In the Catholic tradition, sins are categorized into venial and mortal, each carrying its own weight and spiritual consequences. Mortal sins, by nature, lead to eternal separation from God if not absolved. But what of those sins regarded as unforgivable directly by Scripture and theology?

The notion of certain sins being beyond the reach of divine forgiveness is primarily rooted in Christ's own words in the Gospel of Matthew: "And so I tell you, every kind of sin and slander can be forgiven, but blasphemy against the Spirit will not be forgiven." (Matthew 12:31). This verse forms the underpinning of what has come to be known as the "unforgivable sin." Over centuries, scholars have debated its precise meaning. Does this speak to a specific act or, more fundamentally, to a state of heart so hardened that it refuses the grace offered?

Saint Alphonsus Liguori's theological musings provide significant insights into this moral conundrum. He proposed that sins become unforgivable not due to God's unwillingness to pardon but because the sinner places themselves beyond the reach of forgiveness by rejecting the grace of contrition. This interpretation leads us to ponder the delicate balance between divine justice and mercy. If, at the moment of death, an individual possesses even the smallest trace of repentance, can that engender hope for absolution?

Modern moral theology often aligns itself with Liguori's stance, contending that it's not the sin itself that clinches one's eternal fate, but the sinner's obstinate refusal to repent. Such refusal is seen as the sin against the Holy Spirit: a willful turning away from God's mercy. Thus, the "unforgivable" nature of the sin pivots not on the sin's inherent evilness but on the sinner's adamant disposition.

Yet, documented cases throughout Church history reveal how this theological principle has been interpreted and applied differently across eras and cultures. From the early Church fathers who grappled with apostasies and betrayals to medieval canonists codifying penances, the view shifted reflecting the evolving understanding of human psychology and divine clemency. The Church's extensive canonical writings, pastoral letters, and theological treatises chronicle a long-standing effort to navigate these treacherous waters.

- Is blasphemy against the Spirit uniquely damning because it negates the fundamental principle of repentance?
- Could there exist a state of soul so unyielding that divine grace is rendered ineffective?

These are not questions with easy answers. In fact, they remain under active discussion among theologians. One practical contemporary implication of this debate involves pastoral approaches to confession and absolution. How should a confessor address a penitent who expresses fear of having committed an unforgivable sin? Here, the doctrine of imperfect contrition becomes particularly relevant. Unlike perfect contrition, which arises out of pure love of God, imperfect contrition is born out of a fear of damnation. Despite its seeming inadequacy, it remains sufficient for God's mercy when coupled with sacramental confession.

Exploring deeper into ecclesiastical records and liturgical practices reveals another layer to this discourse. The sacrament of confession itself has evolved, aligned inextricably with the Church's perception of sin and forgiveness. Originally a public and often severe penance transitioned to the more private and pastoral form we recognize today. This shift underscores a more profound appreciation of God's boundless mercy and a reaffirmation that the door to repentance is never truly closed for those willing to knock.

Thus, the struggle continues. Moral theologians and canon lawyers alike engage in intricate examinations of textual and historical contexts, seeking clarity. In their searches, stories of saints and sinners too, fortify this theological journey with vivid, often poignant testimonials. Consider St. Maria Goretti who, on her deathbed, forgave her murderer—an astonishing testament to mercy's transformative power.

The essence of these debates rest on two contrasting images: Divine Justice and Divine Mercy. Divine Justice demands reparation and upholds the moral order. Conversely, Divine Mercy transcends human failings, offering a path through repentance. The apparent tension between these two attributes form the crux of discussions on the unforgivable sin.

As we conclude our examination, it's crucial to understand that the journey is not just intellectual but also deeply spiritual and pastoral. Moral theologians must wield compassion as they traverse this complex landscape, embedding their directives with the profound love and mercy that characterizes Divine essence. While some sins seem insurmountable, Catholic doctrine consistently leans toward hope and conversion.

In this light, the so-called "unforgivable sin" becomes less about divine limitation and more about human choice. When one persistently rejects the Holy Spirit's nudge toward repentance, one tragically places oneself outside the bounds of salvation. However, as long as there's breath within, the Church holds that the possibility of repentance and redemption remains.

The question of whether some sins are truly unforgivable is not merely a theological puzzle but a profound dive into the human soul's capacities for despair and hope. As moral theology continues to evolve, it does so with the unwavering belief in God's infinite mercy, ever ready to embrace the repentant heart.

Chapter 9: Case Studies in Incomplete Contrition

In the annals of moral theology, case studies serve as the crucible where doctrines are tested and lived human experiences unfold. Examining instances of incomplete contrition reveals the nuanced interplay between theological principles and the exigencies of real-life penitence. From medieval confessions recorded by ecclesiastical scribes to modern tales of moral uncertainty, these cases illuminate the struggle between fear and love, remorse and repentance. Consider a 13th-century knight returning from crusade, battling not only physical scars but spiritual ones, seeking absolution yet wrestling with pride. Contrast that with a contemporary case—a corporate executive embroiled in ethical lapses, plagued by guilt yet clinging to worldly fears. Each narrative underscores the Church's enduring challenge: to untangle the web of human frailty and guide souls towards reconciliation, even when contrition remains imperfect. Thus, these case studies aren't merely chronicles; they are mirrors reflecting the relentless pursuit of divine mercy amidst the imperfections of human contrition.

Historical Cases

The annals of ecclesiastical history are rife with dramatic and poignant cases that illustrate the intricacies of incomplete contrition. These narratives often serve not only as moral and theological benchmarks but also as fascinating windows into the complexities of human nature. Exploring historical cases allows us to grasp the lived experiences behind doctrinal formulations and brings into sharp focus the tension between divine justice and mercy.

One significant case that has preoccupied theologians for centuries took place during the early medieval period. The subject was a wayward monk, Brother Reginald, who found himself embroiled in the sin of avarice. Despite his repeated acts of penance, Reginald could never summon the inner fervor of perfect contrition. His fear of divine punishment was his primary motivator, casting a cloud over the efficacy of his penance. It wasn't until he lay on his deathbed, with his brethren praying over him, that he reportedly had a transformative experience, feeling a blend of fear and profound love that seemed to render his contrition more complete. Nevertheless, this case served as a pivotal study in understanding where the line between perfect and imperfect contrition might blur.

Moving forward in time, the case of the repentant king, King David of Israel, stands as an Old Testament narrative often revisited in this discourse. David's grievous sins of adultery and murder, followed by a profound outpouring of repentance, epitomized the ideal of perfect contrition. However, scholars have debated whether David's initial contrition was spurred more by the terror of God's punishment, as delivered by the prophet Nathan, than by genuine penitence. Historical records show that David's lamentations in the Psalms capture a wide range of emotions—fear, sorrow, and love for God—offering rich material for moral theologians to analyze the complex nuances of contritional states.

Transitioning to the Renaissance period, the case of Girolamo Savonarola, an Italian Dominican friar, contributed significantly to the discourse on incomplete contrition. Known for his fiery sermons and strict adherence to moral reform, Savonarola himself faced excommunication and execution. His final moments were reportedly filled with profound repentance, colored by both fear and a fervent appeal to divine mercy. Savonarola's case remains a touchstone for discussions around the efficacy of incomplete contrition, especially under the duress of imminent death.

In the Baroque period, the life and confessions of the infamous highwayman, Claude Duval, offer yet another compelling case study. Duval's criminal exploits made him a notorious figure, but his final days were marked by claims of genuine repentance. His initial contrition seemed driven more by fear of eternal damnation than by a love for God. Yet, theologians have often cited his final moments, where he expressed a deep sorrow for his sins and an appeal to divine mercy, as a turning point from mere imperfect contrition to potentially more perfect contrition.

The records from the Counter-Reformation include the influential case of Maria Magdalene de' Pazzi, a Carmelite mystic. Her confessions, steeped in mystical experiences, often blurred the lines between fear-induced contrition and love-fueled repentance. Her case became pivotal in examining the subjective experiences that contribute to contrition's completeness. Her spiritual diaries reveal an oscillation between terror of divine retribution and a profound love for God, offering fertile ground for theologians contemplating the gray areas between imperfect and perfect contrition.

In the 19th century, a well-documented case involves that of Oscar Wilde, an author and playwright whose life was marked by scandal and eventual imprisonment. Wilde's later writings, particularly "De Profundis," reveal a soul in torment, grappling with his sins and expressing a complex form of repentance. His contrition appeared more imperfect, driven by the fear of social and divine consequences, but his heartfelt appeals to God's mercy invoked questions about the transformative potential of even an incomplete contrition. Wilde's case continues to be a rich vein for exploring how human experiences and emotions interplay in the realm of contrition.

In more recent history, the case of Dietrich Bonhoeffer, a German pastor and theologian executed by the Nazis, introduced layers of complexity to contrition borne out of extreme circumstances. Though not traditionally aligned with Roman Catholic doctrines, Bonhoeffer's letters and writings from prison depicted a soul deeply penitent, yet clearly fearful of both earthly and divine judgment. His case forces a reevaluation of contrition's dimensions amid severe existential threats.

Each case challenges preconceived notions about the nature of contrition, illustrating that the human soul's journey towards repentance is far from linear. Fear, love, despair, and hope are inexorably interwoven in these narratives, providing depth and texture to our understanding of contrition's nature. Theologians have long debated how these multifaceted emotional states align with or fall short of the Church's teachings on complete and incomplete contrition.

In analyzing these historical cases, one must appreciate the sociocultural contexts that shaped each individual's journey of repentance.

The fear of hellfire and divine wrath was palpable in medieval and Renaissance Europe, just as the existential dread found in the modern era has colored contemporary understandings of sin and repentance. By studying these cases, moral theologians and canon lawyers gain invaluable insights into the lived realities behind doctrinal tenets, enabling a more compassionate and nuanced pastoral approach.

Ultimately, these narratives underscore the profound complexity and humanity inherent in the act of repentance. They serve as a reminder that while the Church provides a doctrinal framework, the lived experience of contrition can often transcend neat theological categorizations. Historical cases illuminate the necessity for an empathetic and context-sensitive application of doctrines concerning contrition, and they remind us of the enduring struggle between our human frailties and the divine ideal.

Modern Applications

The intricacies of incomplete contrition, as deeply rooted in Catholic theology, present modern challenges that theologians, confessors, and the faithful cannot ignore. Emerging from centuries of theological debate and doctrinal development, incomplete contrition has seen varied interpretations and applications, particularly in today's rapidly changing moral landscape. Imperfect contrition—especially when it arises from the fear of Hell rather than the love of God—poses significant questions for contemporary pastoral care and canon law.

In our modern era, people face moral quandaries never before encountered by earlier generations. Technological advancements, social changes, and evolving cultural norms introduce complex moral scenarios that often complicate traditional understandings of sin and contrition. Moreover, the anonymity provided by technology has both heightened awareness of sin and simultaneously desensitized many to its severity, making genuine contrition, even if imperfect, a rare occurrence in some cases.

The Sacrament of Confession, while fundamentally unchanged, operates within a new paradigm today. Priests often encounter penitents who struggle with moral confusion or express contrition in ways that reflect contemporary anxieties and pressures. These modern penitents might wrestle with sins that range from internet addiction to bioethical violations—issues that classical moral theology did not address in detail. Therefore, confessors need to possess a nuanced understanding of both the timeless principles of contrition and the contemporary contexts in which these principles are applied.

When addressing modern applications of incomplete contrition, one must not overlook the influence of global interconnectedness. The exchange of cultural values has led some individuals to reassess their understanding of sin, guilt, and repentance. In many parts of the world, the concept of sin has been heavily influenced by secular ideologies, which often downplay the gravity of moral failings. As a result, the contemporary Church faces the challenge of re-educating the faithful on the seriousness of sin and the necessity of at least imperfect contrition for forgiveness.

One pertinent case study involves the moral dilemmas faced by healthcare professionals today. Consider a Catholic physician torn between the demands of their profession, such as participating in procedures that contravene Church teachings, and their religious convictions. Confession for these individuals often includes an element of imperfect contrition, driven by professional duty and societal pressure rather than perfect charity. The confessor's role in such instances is not merely to absolve but to guide the penitent toward a fuller understanding and practice of perfect contrition.

Also, digital platforms provide new avenues for contrition but come with their own set of challenges. Online confession services, though controversial and not officially recognized by the Church, nonetheless reflect a society yearning for remote solutions to spiritual needs. While they may offer convenience, they may also further the issue of incomplete contrition by reducing the sacrament to a transactional interaction rather than a profound moment of grace. Thus, these services risk diluting the essential transformative nature of the sacrament.

In educational settings, Catholic universities and institutions also grapple with modern interpretations of contrition. Young adults, often exposed to a moral relativism that challenges absolute truths, find it difficult to form a contrition rooted in perfect love of God. Educational programs need to emphasize the development of a well-formed conscience, focusing on the importance of recognizing the horror of sin in light of God's infinite goodness, and less so on the self-centered fear of eternal damnation.

Furthermore, businesses rooted in Catholic social teaching face unique challenges in nurturing an environment where true contrition is encouraged. Ethical business practices, corporate social responsibility, and the reconciliation of profits with moral good demand leaders who model contrition and forgiveness. These business leaders must navigate the complexities of modern capitalist economies while ensuring their practices align with the humility and sincerity required for contrition, avoiding the pitfall of seeing repentance merely as a means to repair professional reputation rather than genuine moral reconciliation with God.

In modern psychiatric practice, the differentiation between psychological guilt and theological contrition is particularly significant. Psychiatrists and counselors often deal with clients who experience profound guilt that stems from moral failings. For these individuals, the journey to contrition may require navigating the muddy waters of emotional and spiritual turmoil. The role of Catholic pastoral care, intertwined with mental health interventions, creates a holistic approach addressing both the spiritual necessity for contrition and the psychological need for healing.

Catechesis and ongoing faith formation, tailored to modern needs, play crucial roles in nurturing a deeper understanding of contrition among the laity. Parish programs and diocesan initiatives must adopt innovative approaches to teach about sin, grace, and forgiveness in ways that resonate with contemporary experiences. Through effective catechesis, both children and adults can learn to balance the fear of God with an authentic love for Him, fostering conditions where imperfect contrition can gradually evolve into perfect contrition.

Finally, it is imperative to consider the Pope's role in addressing incomplete contrition in the modern age. Papal encyclicals and apostolic exhortations have continuously evolved to meet the spiritual needs of the time. Documents such as "Misericordiae Vultus" and initiatives like the Year of Mercy stand as testaments to the Church's commitment to highlighting the necessity of mercy, pardon, and the opportunities for grace that penitents have, even when their contrition is imperfect.

In summary, modern applications of incomplete contrition reveal a complex interplay between traditional theological principles and contemporary moral challenges. The task for the Church is not only to uphold the doctrines surrounding contrition but to contextualize them within the lived experiences of today's faithful. This endeavor requires a balanced approach, integrating sound catechesis, compassionate pastoral care, and a keen awareness of the moral realities that characterize our current era.

Chapter 10: The Role of Grace in Contrition

The mysterious dance between divine grace and human contrition lies at the core of Catholic soteriology. Grace, as the Church fathers posited, isn't merely an external aid but a transformative force that penetrates the very fabric of the penitent's soul. While contrition, whether perfect or imperfect, is a visible sign of remorse and a rejection of sin, it's grace that elevates this repentance from a mere human endeavor into a spiritual renewal. When a soul, weighed down by the gravity of its transgressions, encounters the light of divine grace, an intricate synergy unfolds. This interaction does not undermine free will; instead, it enhances it, enabling the penitent to navigate the murky waters of guilt and shame towards the serene shores of forgiveness. In the shadowy alleys of the confessional, grace becomes the guiding lantern, illuminating the path from despair to hope, from sin to redemption, demonstrating that it is through divine assistance that true contrition achieves its salvific potential.

Divine Grace and Human Response

In the intricate dance between human frailty and divine benevolence, the concept of grace holds a position of unparalleled significance. Grace, understood as the free and unmerited favor of God, serves as the bedrock upon which the entire edifice of contrition is constructed. Within Catholic theology, grace acts as both an initiator and sustainer of the journey towards genuine repentance. It woos, compels, and guides the penitent heart, orchestrating a harmonious symphony between the divine and the human.

To comprehend the depth of divine grace, one must acknowledge its multi-faceted nature. Grace is both prevenient and sanctifying. Prevenient grace precedes human decision, nudging the soul towards the goodness it naturally resists due to original sin. Sanctifying grace, on the other hand, dwells within the soul, illuminating the path of righteousness and rendering the contrite heart worthy of absolution. These two expressions of grace illustrate how God's benevolence remains ever-active in the process of contrition, ensuring that human agency never operates in a vacuum.

Historically, the Catholic Church has articulated the interplay of divine grace and human response through the teachings of theologians like Saint Augustine and Saint Thomas Aquinas. Augustine emphasized the necessity of grace for any good action, asserting that even the first movement towards repentance is a result of divine intervention. Aquinas elaborated on this by distinguishing between actual grace (which acts at specific moments to inspire good actions) and habitual grace (which remains within the soul, influencing its continuous orientation towards God).

The role of divine grace is not to override human free will but to work synergistically with it. This synergy is crucial in the context of contrition, where human repentance meets divine forgiveness. Without grace, the heart remains hard and unyielding. With grace, the possibility of true contrition, whether perfect or imperfect, becomes a tangible reality. Grace gently opens the heart, enabling it to recognize its need for God and to respond with a sorrow that is genuine, albeit imperfect at times.

Consider the dichotomy between perfect and imperfect contrition, a concept richly explored in the Church's teachings. Perfect contrition arises out of pure love for God, sorrow for sin being motivated by the recognition of having offended divine love. Imperfect contrition, however, stems from a fear of divine retribution or the ugliness of sin itself. Despite its lesser purity, imperfect contrition remains valid and efficacious insofar as it opens the door to God's grace, pushing the soul toward the sacrament of confession.

One might wonder about the moral tension inherent in this spectrum of contrition. How can imperfect contrition, driven by self-centered fear rather than divine love, still be of value in the eyes of the Church? Herein lies the transformative power of grace. Divine grace does not discriminate based on the initial quality of repentance. Instead, it sanctifies and elevates the penitent heart, gradually transforming imperfect contrition into perfect love through the continuous influx of divine assistance.

St. Alphonsus Liguori's teachings underscore this transformative aspect of grace. Liguori posits that God's grace is most abundantly available in the sacraments, particularly confession, where it purifies the penitent's intentions. This purification occurs even if the penitent initially approaches the sacrament with imperfect contrition. Grace perfects, completes, and makes holy what human effort alone cannot achieve.

In real-life pastoral applications, confessors are often mediators of this divine grace. They provide spiritual guidance and help the faithful to recognize the workings of grace in their lives. Through the confessor's counsel, the penitent can better perceive how divine grace has been operative even in their imperfect sorrow. This awareness fosters deeper repentance and a renewed commitment to spiritual growth.

It is worth noting that the sacraments themselves are tangible channels of grace. In confession, grace not only prompts sorrow for sin but also offers the strength to resist future temptation and sin. The absolution pronounced by the priest is a divine act, extending God's grace to sweep away the spiritual detritus that clings to the penitent soul.

The relationship between grace and free will is complex. Some might argue that an overemphasis on grace diminishes human responsibility. Yet, the Church maintains that while grace is a divine gift, human response remains essential. Free will, enlightened and assisted by grace, must cooperate with God's will to achieve genuine conversion. This cooperation is neither passive nor automatic. It requires an active, intentional response from the human heart.

In examining this dynamic, contemporary theologians have likened it to a dance, where divine grace leads and human response follows. The freedom of the will is respected, yet always invited to yield to the gentle yet persistent promptings of grace. This dance reaches its crescendo in acts of perfect contrition but remains valuable even in its imperfect forms.

One key aspect of this interplay is the recognition of human imperfections. While the ultimate aim is perfect contrition, God's grace meets individuals where they are. This means that even those who struggle with deep-rooted fears or habitual sins can still find a path to reconciliation, illuminated by grace. The journey towards perfect contrition might be long and fraught with setbacks, but divine grace ensures that every step taken is a step towards the divine.

The theological concept of synergy between divine grace and human response ultimately affirms the mercy and patience of God. He does not demand immediate perfection but lovingly works within the confines of human weakness. Grace is the catalyst that allows the penitent to move closer to God's ideal of perfect love and contrition.

In conclusion, the intersection of divine grace and human response in the context of contrition is a profound testament to God's unwavering love and mercy. It highlights the continuous outpouring of divine grace, which meets the human soul in its moments of sorrow and transforms it, leading it gently yet resolutely towards true repentance. It is a dance of divine love and human freedom, orchestrated by a God who desires not just our contrition but our ultimate sanctification.

The Interplay between Free Will and Divine Assistance

The proportions of free will and divine assistance are at the heart of understanding the role of grace in contrition. Here, we must confront the age-old question: How do human agency and divine grace collaborate in the process of repentance within the Catholic framework? The tension between these two forces is not merely theoretical; it fundamentally influences how we approach sin, contrition, and ultimately, forgiveness.

In Catholic theology, free will is paramount. Human beings are endowed with the capacity to choose freely between good and evil, making them morally accountable for their actions. This intrinsic capacity for choice is indispensable for genuine contrition and repentance. Without free will, contrition would be coerced and therefore lacking in authenticity. However, the Church also teaches that human effort alone is inadequate for true repentance; divine grace must play a role. This duality forms the crucible within which the drama of salvation unfolds.

Divine assistance, often elaborated upon through the concept of grace, acts as the enabler and sustainer of human will in the act of contrition. Grace is believed to be a divine favor bestowed upon individuals, enabling them to accomplish what would be humanly impossible — namely, turning their hearts towards God. The interplay between free will and divine grace thus necessitates a cooperative interaction. This partnership does not diminish human responsibility; rather, it under-scores the indispensable role of divine help in moral and spiritual growth.

To delve deeper, we must consider the different types of grace: actual grace and sanctifying grace. Actual grace is transient and is given for specific circumstances to guide a person towards a particular action, like the moment of genuine repentance. Sanctifying grace, on the other hand, is a stable condition of being that endows the soul with the divine life necessary to sustain a virtuous existence. The orchestration of these graces in aligning the human will towards genuine contrition reflects a nuanced dance where divine action and human freedom elegantly interlace.

Consider the doctrine of prevenient grace, which posits that no one can even begin to seek God without God's initial, enabling action. This preemptive grace illuminates the path to repentance, yet it does not force us to walk it. We retain our autonomy, our freedom to respond to or reject God's invitation to repent. It's this delicate balance that Saint Augustine captured when he said, "He that created us without our help will not save us without our consent."

In the intricate relationship between free will and divine assistance, some might argue that the scales tip towards divine grace, making human effort seem inconsequential. However, the Catholic Church stands firm on the importance of human cooperation with divine grace. This cooperation is crucial for authentic contrition as well as for the sacraments, particularly the Sacrament of Confession. The penitent must make a conscious, willing effort to receive forgiveness, illustrating that while divine assistance is vital, it does not override or nullify human free will.

Notably, Saint Alphonsus Liguori, a significant voice in moral the-ology, elaborated on this interaction extensively. He argued that God's grace is always offered but human beings must freely accept it. Liguori emphasized the necessity of human cooperation through acts of con-fession, penance, and a genuine intention to amend one's life. His teachings illuminate how divine assistance facilitates but does not force contrition. Thus, free will is exercised within the framework of divine grace, allowing the individual to partake in the transformative power of repentance.

This dual reliance is not without its complexities. Imperfect contrition, motivated by a fear of damnation rather than love of God, may seem less reliant on divine grace and more on human self-interest. Yet, even here, divine grace is present, nudging the soul towards repentance. The interplay is such that God meets us where we are, using our natural inclinations and fears to guide us back to Him.

Further complicating matters is the reality of concupiscence — the inclination to sin inherent in human beings. This propensity underscores the necessity of divine assistance, as our free will, though critical, is often weakened by the effects of original sin. The grace provided by the Holy Spirit strengthens the will, enabling imperfect and perfect contrition to take root and bear fruit. In this way, grace not only assists but also heals and elevates our natural capacity for freedom and decision-making.

The theological debates surrounding this topic have been extensive and, at times, contentious. Some argue that too great an emphasis on divine grace might lead to a sort of spiritual complacency, where individuals rely on God to the exclusion of personal responsibility. Others maintain that emphasizing human effort risks promoting a form of Pelagianism, the heretical belief that humans can achieve salvation through their own efforts without divine assistance. The Church navigates between these extremes, advocating a synergistic relationship where divine grace and human free will co-operate in the journey towards God.

Finally, while the theological intricacies are profound, the pastoral implications are equally significant. In the confessional, a priest acts as an intermediary, dispensing the grace of the sacrament while also guiding the penitent to an understanding of their own free will's role in repentance. It is an encounter where both elements — divine assistance and human freedom — must be acknowledged and integrated.

In summation, the interplay between free will and divine assistance is a dynamic and complex relationship that underpins the Catholic understanding of contrition and repentance. It is a dance of divine grace and human freedom, where each relies on and elevates the other. In this profound interaction lies the essence of Catholic moral theology, a testament to the eternal cooperation between God's guiding hand and our willing hearts.

Chapter 11: Ecclesiastical and Canonical Perspectives

As we turn to the ecclesiastical and canonical perspectives on contrition and confession, it becomes evident that the Church's doctrine is not merely theological but also deeply enshrined in its laws and teachings. Canon Law, through its specified canons, meticulously delineates the requirements for genuine contrition and the sacrament of confession. It ensures that these acts are not hollow rituals, but transformative experiences aligning with ecclesial decrees. The Church, through various councils and papal encyclicals, has consistently underscored the importance of both perfect and imperfect contrition while emphasizing the indispensable role of confession for absolution. This dual emphasis on legal structure and spiritual doctrine reflects a holistic approach—one that integrates the strictness of law with the grace of divine mercy, ensuring the faithful not only adhere to the sacramental protocol but also genuinely seek reconciliation with God. This intricate tapestry of law and grace, doctrine, and pastoral care, reveals the Church's commitment to guiding souls towards true repentance and ultimate salvation.

Canon Law on Contrition and Confession

In exploring the intricacies of canon law as it relates to the concepts of contrition and confession, one must delve deeply into the principles that underpin the Catholic Church's legal framework. The governance of souls through juridical means captures an element of divine justice, interwoven with mercy and penitence. The tight rope walked by ecclesiastical law is indeed one of balance—between the demands of upholding moral order and the pastoral mission to save souls.

Canon law systematically addresses contrition and confession primarily in the Code of Canon Law promulgated in 1983. The canons elucidate the requirements and faculties necessary for the valid and licit administration of the Sacrament of Penance. Intriguingly, this legal codex provides a robust architecture, detailing not only the necessities for absolution but also the dispositions required of penitents seeking reconciliation.

Crucial to understanding these regulations is the distinction between perfect and imperfect contrition. Perfect contrition, motivated by the love of God, and imperfect contrition, stemming from a fear of punishment, both serve as valid precursors to confession. Though the former is superior in its purity of motive, the latter is sufficient within the sacramental context under canon law.

Canon 960 stands central to any discussion on confession, stipulating that individual and integral confession and absolution constitute the sole ordinary means by which a member of the faithful conscious of grave sin is reconciled with God and the Church. This provision underscores the essential role of the sacrament in the moral and spiritual lives of the faithful.

Where the penitent's disposition comes into play, we encounter Canon 987, which mandates true contrition as a fundamental requirement for a valid confession. The penitent must be sorrowful for their sins out of moral conviction and determined not to commit them again. The Church, via its canonical statutes, thus emphasizes an authentic conversion of heart, reflecting a journey towards spiritual maturity and moral rectitude.

Another critical aspect is the role of the priest, acting in persona Christi, as he administers the sacrament. Canon 965 clarifies that only a priest is the minister of the sacrament of penance. The priest's faculties for hearing confessions are granted canonically and require appropriate jurisdiction, as elucidated in Canon 966. This ensures consistency and adherence to established norms across dioceses and ecclesiastical jurisdictions.

Practically, Canon 980 prescribes that if the confessor has no doubt about the penitent's dispositions and the penitent seeks absolution, absolution should not be refused or deferred. This canon acts as a safeguard against arbitrary or unjust denial of the sacrament, promoting an emphasis on God's mercy.

Penalty and reconciliation converge within Canon 986, which obligates priests to make themselves available to the faithful seeking confession, particularly those in danger of death. This emphasizes the pastoral urgency and duty to administer God's grace, regardless of the circumstances, underscoring the salvific nature of the Church's mission.

Delving further, Canon 988 addresses the confessional obligation of the faithful to confess all grave sins in kind and number, reflecting the theological underpinning that genuine sorrow and clear articulation of one's sins are vital for absolution. This precision aims to combat complacency and ensure the penitent's comprehensive examination of conscience.

In conjunction, Canon 989 provides the normative duty for the faithful to confess serious sins at least once a year. This canon underlines the Church's role in facilitating regular spiritual accountability and encourages a habit of ongoing repentance.

Nota bene, the Church makes provision for extraordinary forms of reconciliation under specific conditions, delineated in Canon 961. In cases of imminent death or grave necessity, general absolution without prior individual confession can be administered. This underscores the pragmatic flexibility of canon law while maintaining its moral rigor.

It is timely to recall the Church's provision for "internal forum" solutions—confidential decisions made in the confessional concerning one's personal relationship with God. These often profound and complex cases are guided by both pastoral concern and canonical mandates, aiming to balance justice with mercy.

To conclude, canon law on contrition and confession is a testament to the Catholic Church's commitment to uphold doctrinal purity while extending pastoral care. It navigates the human condition's myriad complexities through a framework that seeks to restore each soul to grace within the bounds of legal and moral order. In offering the sacrament of reconciliation, the Church not only adjudicates sin but also embraces the sinner, inviting a renewal of life in Christ.

Ecclesiastical Teachings and Decrees

The ecclesiastical teachings and decrees of the Catholic Church have long served as the bedrock for understanding sin, contrition, and reconciliation. The Church's stance on these issues reflects centuries of theological thought, pastoral care, and doctrinal development. At the heart of this complex edifice lies a web of principles and regulations designed to guide the faithful toward salvation while ensuring the integrity of the Church's sacramental framework. In particular, the tension between unforgivable sins and imperfect contrition necessitates a detailed exploration of these teachings and decrees.

One fundamental ecclesiastical teaching concerns the delineation between mortal and venial sins. This distinction is not merely theoretical but plays a critical role in how the sacraments function. Mortal sins, possessing the gravitas to sever one's relationship with God, underscore the necessity of contrition and confession. On the other hand, venial sins, while damaging, do not destroy divine friendship. Ecclesiastical decrees provide a roadmap for navigating these moral landscapes, dictating the proper form and intention required for the sacrament of confession to be valid.

The Church has consistently emphasized the importance of perfect contrition—sorrow for sin out of love for God—as the ideal form of repentance. Yet, acknowledging human frailty, it also permits imperfect contrition—sorrow driven by fear of divine punishment—as a valid foundation for confession. The intrinsic difference between these forms of contrition is subtle yet significant, informing pastoral practices and guiding confessional protocols. Decrees such as the Council of Trent have explicitly confirmed that imperfect contrition, while not the purest form of repentance, suffices for the sacrament of confession if it encompasses a genuine intention to amend one's ways.

Integral to understanding ecclesiastical teachings is the role of canon law. These legal standards codify the Church's moral and sacramental requirements, ensuring uniformity and clarity in ecclesiastical matters. Canon Law meticulously outlines the prerequisites for valid confessions, including the necessity for contrition, confession of sins, and satisfaction. Particularly, Canon 959 encapsulates the essence of the sacrament: the penitent must confess to a priest, expressing sincere sorrow and a firm purpose of amendment. The symbiotic relationship between ecclesiastical teachings and canonical decrees fosters a holistic approach to sin and repentance.

The historical evolution of ecclesiastical decrees concerning confession reflects the Church's response to heretical movements, pastoral needs, and theological developments. For instance, the early Church's penitential practices were initially public and often severe. Over time, these evolved into private and more personal forms of confession, influenced by monastic traditions and the Fourth Lateran Council's decree in 1215, which mandated annual confession for all Christians. Such developments illustrate the dynamic interplay between doctrine and pastoral application, always aiming to balance justice with mercy.

Ecclesiastical teachings also extend to the administration of absolution. The priest, acting in persona Christi, exercises the power of binding and loosing granted by Christ to His apostles. This authority is not merely symbolic but is fortified by rigorous theological underpinnings and ecclesiastical endorsement. The priest's role involves not only hearing confessions but also discerning the genuineness of the penitent's contrition, thereby determining the appropriateness of absolution.

Herein lies the pastoral wisdom enshrined within ecclesiastical decrees, designed to safeguard the sacrament's sanctity.

Moreover, ecclesiastical decrees have robustly addressed the notion of "unforgivable sin," primarily the sin against the Holy Spirit. According to Church teachings, this sin involves a willful and obstinate rejection of God's mercy and grace, rendering forgiveness impossible—not because of a limitation in divine mercy but due to the penitent's hardened heart. Such teachings underscore the gravity of deliberate and unrepentant sin, reinforcing the necessity for genuine contrition as a precondition for forgiveness. By codifying these principles in official decrees, the Church underscores the crucial balance between divine justice and mercy.

In reinforcing these doctrines, the Church has also promulgated indulgences as a means to alleviate the temporal punishment due to sin. These ecclesiastical mechanisms, deeply rooted in the Church's penitential system, highlight the transformative power of grace. Indulgences, whether partial or plenary, are granted under specific conditions and require a contrite heart. Such decrees not only foster a deeper understanding of grace and repentance but also encourage the faithful towards a life of piety and devotion.

The ecclesiastical body has also promulgated teachings concerning the effects of contrition and the role of penance. Penance, as a sacramental act, goes beyond mere reparation; it signifies a spiritual transformation and renewal. Through acts of penance—prayers, good works, or other forms of mortification—the penitent demonstrates a commitment to amend their life, thereby actualizing the grace received through absolution. As these teachings weave through the ecclesiastical fabric, they form a cohesive framework that addresses the multifaceted nature of human sinfulness and divine forgiveness.

Ecclesiastical decrees also emphasize the safeguarding of the sacramental seal of confession. The inviolability of the confessional is a cornerstone of the Church's commitment to providing a safe sanctuary for the penitent. Any violation of this seal attracts severe canonical penalties, reinforcing the sacredness of the confessional space. This unwavering stance underscores the Church's dedication to upholding the penitent's trust and the sacrament's integrity. By maintaining absolute confidentiality, the Church ensures the penitent's unburdened disclosure of sins, facilitating genuine reconciliation.

Through a tapestry of teachings and decrees, the Church articulates its stance on contrition, confession, and absolution. These ecclesiastical principles are not static; they evolve, reflecting the Church's response to new challenges and deeper theological insights. By continually revisiting and refining these teachings, the Church endeavors to offer coherent guidance, resonating with timeless truths while addressing contemporary concerns. Such dynamic interaction between established doctrine and pastoral application epitomizes the Church's mission to lead the faithful towards spiritual wholeness and salvation.

In conclusion, the ecclesiastical teachings and decrees surrounding contrition, confession, and absolution encapsulate a profound theological and pastoral heritage. They navigate the delicate balance between justice and mercy, sin and redemption, imperfection, and divine grace. For moral theologians, Roman Catholics, and Canon lawyers, these teachings provide a critical framework for understanding the Church's sacramental praxis and doctrinal convictions. Embedded within this continuum of ecclesiastical wisdom is the enduring message of hope and reconciliation, inviting all towards the transformative embrace of God's mercy.

Chapter 12: Contemporary Challenges

In the labyrinthine corridors of modern moral theology, contemporary challenges present themselves with a weight that rivals that of bygone eras. Pastoral approaches to imperfect contrition have shifted in response to the evolving intricacies of human behavior and conscience. The Church, steadfast in her traditions, now faces newfound dilemmas that compel a reevaluation of established doctrines. Canon lawyers and theologians are tasked with navigating these tumultuous waters, where the penitent's imperfect contrition grapples with an unforgiving societal landscape. Whether addressing moral relativism or the digital age's confounding influence, the tightrope walks between tradition and modernity with a finesse that requires both doctrinal fidelity and pastoral sensitivity. Strategies are forged in the crucible of engagement, empathy, and unwavering commitment to the sacrament's sanctity, ever mindful of the eternal truths handed down through centuries.

Pastoral Approaches to Imperfect Contrition

Understanding and addressing imperfect contrition is a contemporary challenge facing the Catholic Church. Imperfect contrition, which arises more from fear of divine punishment than from a love of God, presents unique pastoral concerns. Given that perfect contrition, driven by love for God, remains the ideal, the Church must navigate a delicate balance in guiding the faithful toward authentic repentance, without alienating those who come forward with less-than-perfect contrition.

Pastorally, the Church acknowledges human frailty and the reality that sinners might not always possess perfect contrition. However, the sacrament of Confession offers a vital avenue for grace. Priests must, therefore, convey the understanding that while imperfect contrition suffices for absolution, it opens the door to a journey toward deeper spiritual conversion.

Effective pastoral approaches require priests to evaluate the disposition of the penitent empathetically. The priest's role extends beyond mere absolution to being a spiritual guide. Encouraging penitents through compassionate dialogue can transform imperfect contrition into a stepping stone towards perfect contrition.

Furthermore, contemporary moral theologians and canon lawyers underscore the necessity of nuanced catechesis. Educational efforts must elucidate the nature of contrition and its requirements. Emphasizing the supremacy of God's mercy helps penitents embrace the sacrament with openness rather than reluctance, fostering environments where imperfect contrition can gradually evolve.

In an era of moral relativism and declining religious observance, the Church faces the challenge of rekindling a sense of sin and contrition within the contemporary conscience. This requires pastoral creativity and adaptability. Clergy and lay leaders must employ innovative methods—engaging homilies, retreats, and digital platforms—to make the concepts of sin, contrition, and God's mercy accessible and relevant.

Another crucial pastoral approach is fostering communal support within parishes. When communities actively support each other in their faith journeys, individual experiences of God's mercy strengthen collective piety. This support network can be instrumental in helping individuals move from imperfect to perfect contrition through shared prayers, reflections, and spiritual companionship.

Additionally, ecclesial documents and canonical guidance play a pivotal role. Canon law permits absolution with imperfect contrition given the penitent's intent to confess and amend. Such provisions highlight the Church's pragmatism and pastoral sensitivity. Expounding on these provisions in pastoral settings reassures the faithful that the Church understands human limitations.

Yet, the tension between doctrinal purity and pastoral sensitivity remains palpable. Critics argue that too much leniency may dilute the sacrament's significance. Conversely, overly stringent demands risk driving away those in need of grace. Herein lies a pastoral tightrope, requiring shepherds to balance truth and compassion.

Addressing this pastoral challenge also involves moral theologians reassessing and articulating the continuum of contrition. Understanding it not in binary terms but as a dynamic process can reshape pastoral strategies. Such a perspective invites clergy to consider each confession not as a singular event but as part of an ongoing conversion pathway, where imperfect contrition may be the beginning rather than the end.

Moreover, integrating teachings on divine mercy into pastoral care can alleviate the fear that often accompanies imperfect contrition.

Presenting mercy as a fundamental tenet of God's relationship with humanity provides hope. This perspective reshapes contrition from an obligation born of fear to a transformative encounter with divine love.

Lastly, pastoral approaches must remain deeply rooted in prayer. Priests and laity alike should seek divine guidance on how best to minister to those grappling with imperfect contrition. Prayer cultivates a pastoral sensitivity that transcends doctrinal knowledge, enabling clergy to discern the unique needs of each penitent.

In conclusion, addressing imperfect contrition within contemporary pastoral practices requires a multifaceted approach. It blends doctrinal integrity with compassionate sensitivity, communal support with personal catechesis, and an unwavering focus on the transformative power of God's mercy. By doing so, the Church can guide the faithful closer to perfect contrition and, ultimately, a deeper union with God.

Addressing Modern Moral Dilemmas

Modern society presents unique moral dilemmas that challenge both the faithful and the clergy. The rapid pace of technological advancement, shifting social norms, and global interconnectedness contribute to an environment where traditional teachings face unprecedented tests. For theologians, canon lawyers, and pastoral leaders, addressing these dilemmas requires a keen understanding of the Church's moral framework, alongside a compassionate approach to contemporary issues.

At the heart of these challenges is the tension between the unchanging principles of Catholic doctrine and the evolving moral landscape. One glaring area of concern is the application of moral theology in situations that were unimaginable to earlier generations. Assisted reproductive technologies, end-of-life issues, and bioethical questions, for example, each require careful discernment. How does one navigate the sanctity of life when faced with the complexities of modern medicine?

Equally pressing are questions of social justice. As the Church advocates for the dignity of every person, it must also grapple with the moral implications of economic inequality, racial injustice, and political strife. Pastoral leaders are called to guide their communities in reflecting on how Catholic social teaching can be applied in a world marked by stark disparities and suffering.

A significant modern dilemma involves the digital realm. The pervasiveness of social media and the internet introduces questions about privacy, the dissemination of information, and ethical consumption. Priests and lay leaders must help their congregations discern how to live virtuously in an age dominated by screen time and virtual interactions. What does it mean to uphold Christian values in a digital world marred by cyberbullying, misinformation, and unhealthy comparisons?

The Church's teachings on sexual morality and family life also come under intense scrutiny. Issues such as same-sex marriage, divorce, and contraception are hotly debated both within and outside the Church. Pastoral sensitivity is paramount as the Church navigates these sensitive areas while upholding the doctrines that are foundational to its understanding of human nature and divine intention.

There's also the challenge of fostering a genuine understanding of forgiveness and reconciliation in an age that often leans toward punitive measures. In secular society, retribution can overshadow redemption. The Sacrament of Confession is a powerful antidote to this trend, emphasizing God's infinite mercy and the transformative power of grace. Yet, the concept of imperfect contrition — sorrow for sin based on fear of punishment rather than love of God — remains a point of pastoral concern. How can clergy help the faithful move toward more profound contrition?

The complexities of modern family dynamics add another layer. With the rise of blended families, surrogate parenting, and diverse household structures, moral theologians are tasked with providing guidance that is both faithful to Church teachings and sensitive to individual circumstances. How do we offer pastoral care that recognizes the reality of these families while promoting the virtues of fidelity and unity?

Economic issues also present significant moral dilemmas. Global capitalism and consumer culture often lead to situations where the pursuit of profit is prioritized over human dignity and environmental stewardship. The Church's teachings on social justice and the common good are critical here, urging a reevaluation of economic practices that harm individuals and communities. Clarity is needed on how to apply these principles in daily life, from personal financial decisions to corporate ethics.

In addressing these dilemmas, the role of ecclesiastical guidance cannot be overstated. Canon law provides a framework for navigating complex moral issues, yet it must be applied with pastoral wisdom. Canon lawyers and moral theologians work in tandem to interpret and implement these laws in ways that are faithful to Church doctrine and responsive to contemporary needs.

A key pastoral approach involves educational efforts aimed at forming well-informed consciences. Teaching the faithful about the principles of moral theology, the nuances of contrition, and the importance of the Sacrament of Confession helps individuals discern their responsibilities and actions in light of their faith. Contextualizing these teachings in current societal realities makes them more accessible and relevant.

Another important aspect is dialogue. Engaging with the faithful through conversations in parishes, diocesan seminars, and even online platforms promotes understanding and mutual respect. Clergy and lay leaders alike must listen to the real-life experiences and struggles of their communities, fostering an environment where difficult questions can be explored openly and honestly. This approach not only clarifies the Church's teachings but also strengthens the community's commitment to living out their faith.

The concept of "moral dilemma" implies no easy answers, and indeed, many contemporary issues resist simple solutions. However, the consistent emphasis on mercy and love offers a guiding light. In a world often divided by ideology and conflict, the Church's mission to embody and extend Christ's love becomes even more crucial. Addressing modern moral dilemmas, thus, involves not only applying doctrinal teachings but doing so with the empathy and compassion that Jesus himself exemplified.

Ultimately, the challenge lies in balancing doctrinal fidelity with pastoral care. It requires a deep dive into the principles espoused by thinkers like Saint Alphonsus Liguori, whose theological frameworks provide a rich resource for moral discernment. It also calls for a responsive, adaptive engagement with the pressing issues of today, just as those early theologians responded to their own times.

In conclusion, addressing modern moral dilemmas is a multifaceted endeavor that involves theological, pastoral, and practical dimensions. It requires a commitment to the Church's timeless teachings, a sensitivity to the complexities of the contemporary world, and a profound trust in the transformative power of God's grace. By navigating these challenges with both clarity and compassion, the Church continues its mission of guiding the faithful toward holiness and authentic reconciliation with God.

Chapter 13: Divine Mercy

Amidst the dense thickets of moral theology lies a path illuminated by the unwavering light of divine mercy, a concept both devastating and comforting in its magnitude. This chapter ventures into the historical evolution of Divine Mercy, tracing its roots from early Christian thought to the more structured and elaborate indulgences promoted by Saint Faustina Kowalska's revelations in the 20th century. In unraveling the Divine Mercy Indulgence, we confront the profound tension between perfect and imperfect contrition, a dichotomy that bedevils the conscience but offers solace through the boundless love of Christ. As we navigate the intricate relationship between Divine Mercy and contrition, one can't help but reflect on the enigmatic interplay between human frailty and divine benevolence. The essence of Divine Mercy gently insists that even in our most imperfect moments of repentance, there is hope—a steadfast assurance that God's mercy tempers His justice, transcending our finite understanding and bringing healing to the spiritually wounded.

History of Divine Mercy

To understand the history of Divine Mercy, one must delve into the heart of the 20th century where a humble Polish nun, Saint Faustina Kowalska, received a series of visions that would forever transform the Catholic understanding of God's boundless compassion. The Divine Mercy devotion, as we recognize it today, finds its roots in her revelations, which detail a profound message of forgiveness, trust in Jesus, and the limitless mercy of God.

Born in 1905 to a poor but devout family, Helena Kowalska experienced religious visions and a desire to join a convent from an early age. It was not until 1925, after being turned away by various orders due to her lack of dowry and education, that she found the Congregation of the Sisters of Our Lady of Mercy. Within this convent, she assumed the name Faustina and devoted herself to a life of austerity, prayer, and service. It was here, away from the world's recognition, that she began to experience more intense and more frequent visions of Jesus Christ.

In 1931, Faustina reported one of her most momentous visions in which Jesus appeared to her with rays of red and white light streaming from His heart. He instructed her to have an image painted according to this vision, with the inscription "Jesus, I trust in You." This image, now known worldwide, encapsulates the essence of the Divine Mercy message: trust, mercy, and divine love.

Faustina's diary, later compiled into the book "Divine Mercy in My Soul," meticulously details her spiritual encounters and the messages she received. Perhaps the most significant event arose in 1935 when she was inspired to compose the Divine Mercy Chaplet, a prayer dedicated to obtaining mercy for oneself and the entire world. The chaplet has since become an integral part of the devotion, widely recited by the faithful, particularly at 3 o'clock, the "hour of great mercy," marking the traditional hour of Christ's death.

Despite Faustina's early death in 1938 at the age of 33, her legacy was championed by several key figures, most notably Karol Wojtyla, the future Pope John Paul II. He encountered her diaries while he was the Archbishop of Krakow and found profound theological depth and clarity in her messages. As Pope, he canonized Faustina in 2000 and instituted the Feast of Divine Mercy, to be celebrated on the first Sunday after Easter. This feast underscores the aspect of mercy central to Faustina's visions and ties it closely to the Church's liturgical calendar, further embedding it within Catholic tradition.

The theology of Divine Mercy bridges a critical pastoral need, especially when addressing the frailties of human contrition. It recognizes that while perfect contrition — sorrow for sin out of pure love for God — is the ideal, human beings often fall short and possess imperfect contrition — sorrow due to fear of punishment or loss of heaven. Divine Mercy offers an encompassing embrace, providing a refuge for those struggling with feelings of inadequacy in their spiritual lives.

During World War II, as Poland endured severe trials, the message of Divine Mercy offered solace and hope. The Faustina revelations promoted a vision of God not as a stern judge, but as a merciful savior eager to forgive and heal. This considerable shift mirrored the gap between an unforgiving cynicism that was easy to assume given the horrors of war, and the unconditional mercy that Father Maximilian Kolbe symbolized when he offered his life in Auschwitz.

Canonically, Divine Mercy has also influenced ecclesiastical decrees and practices. The late 20th and early 21st centuries saw a renewed emphasis on mercy within the sacrament of confession, with priests encouraged to reflect God's boundless compassion, drawing inspiration from Faustina's revelations. The Church's ongoing re-examination of its approach to pastoral care, especially through the lens of Divine Mercy, underlines the intersection between Heaven's mercy and Earth's need for redemption.

The message of Divine Mercy is not just a historical footnote but a living tradition, actively shaping contemporary theological discourse. It can be seen in papal documents emphasizing reconciliation, synodal discussions about pastoral care, and everyday confessional encounters where the penitent soul finds peace.

Pope Francis, with his bull "Misericordiae Vultus" initiating the Jubilee Year of Mercy in 2016, demonstrated a continuous line of papal affinity towards Divine Mercy. He stressed that mercy is the "beating heart of the Gospel" and the Church must adopt measures to be "a haven of mercy and refuge." Thus, Divine Mercy continues to serve as a lifeline through decades — a vibrant testament that when it comes to sin and contrition, God's mercy remains inexhaustible.

In sum, the history of Divine Mercy is a profound narrative blending mystical revelations, ecclesiastical endorsements, and a perennial call to trust in God's infinite compassion. It challenges and comforts, bridging the doctrinal and the personal, urging believers to place their hope in the Divine Mercy that surpasses human understanding.

The Divine Mercy Indulgence

The concept of the Divine Mercy Indulgence has found its roots deeply embedded in Catholic doctrine, through the revelations given to St. Faustina Kowalska. As a devotion, it is built around the foundation of trust in Jesus Christ's merciful nature and aims to encompass the boundless love and forgiveness that is extended to all repentant sinners. The indulgence serves both as a beacon of hope for those steeped in sin and an illustrative model of the Church's ever-present compassion.

Historically, the Catholic Church has instituted various forms of indulgences to help the faithful alleviate the temporal punishment for sins whose guilt has already been forgiven in the sacrament of confession. The Divine Mercy Indulgence, specific in its own right, highlights the intersection of Divine mercy and ecclesiastical authority. Promulgated with the express wish of Pope John Paul II, the indulgence encapsulates a profound spiritual exercise meant to unite penitents closely with the ultimate sacrifice of Christ.

To understand this indulgence, one must first comprehend the unique conditions under which it is granted. The prerequisites include sacramental confession, Eucharistic communion, and prayer for the intentions of the Holy Father. Additionally, the individual must participate in devotions to the Divine Mercy or perform acts of mercy through deed, word, or prayer. These conditions not only reflect the traditional requirements for any plenary indulgence but also emphasize the distinctive focus on mercy that characterizes this devotion.

Exemplifying the late Pope John Paul II's vision, the Divine Mercy Indulgence serves as a pivotal moment of repentance and reconciliation. The indulgence can be obtained under particular circumstances, especially on Divine Mercy Sunday, the Sunday following Easter. Here, the liturgical calendar aligns to encourage the faithful to turn their gaze upon the "fountain of mercy" that Christ offers. This is not merely an abstract idea but a lived experience within the liturgical life of the Church.

In examining this indulgence through a theological lens, it's crucial to acknowledge that it interlaces with the broader spectrum of Catholic understanding on sin and contrition. The indulgence is a profound testimony to the relationship between divine grace and human cooperation. It underscores the need for true repentance, even when the contrition is imperfect—rooted in the fear of divine justice rather than the pure love of God. Regardless, the mercy of God can bridge these imperfections, leading sinners toward a more profound conversion of heart.

For moral theologians, the Divine Mercy Indulgence offers a critical study on how the doctrines of penance and indulgence coalesce with the omnipresent themes of God's unlimited mercy. It posits that God's mercy does not operate in isolation but through the sacraments and the ecclesiastical authority Christ entrusted to the Church. Thus, the indulgence becomes a touchpoint for discussing the mysterious collaboration between divine efficacy and human agency.

Canon lawyers, too, find fertile ground in the Divine Mercy Indulgence, especially in exploring the codified frameworks that govern its dispensation. Canon law provides structured guidelines that ensure the proper administration of indulgences, reflecting both theological depth and juridical precision. This legal backdrop ensures that the indulgence is not merely an abstract spiritual practice but one grounded in ecclesiastical order and discipline.

The Divine Mercy Indulgence beckons the faithful into a deeper understanding and relationship with the concept of divine mercy. It propels an individual beyond mere ritualistic observance into a heartfelt, transformative encounter with divine grace. When penitents meet the prescribed conditions with sincere repentance, they experience an unparalleled purification, reaffirming the Church's teaching that God's mercy is infinitely greater than any sin.

Practically, the indulgence serves as a testament to how the Church navigates the delicate balance between justice and mercy. It underscores the necessity of satisfaction for sins (satisfaction being one of the three parts of penance, along with contrition and confession) while highlighting that satisfaction itself is facilitated by God's gratuitous grace. This indulgence thus becomes a quintessential example of the Church's pastoral care, seeking the spiritual well-being of its flock.

Examining the Divine Mercy Indulgence within the broader historical and doctrinal landscape of the Church reveals how adaptable yet steadfastly resolute the Church remains in its mission to guide souls towards salvation. When viewed against the Church's storied history with indulgences—some of which have been contentious—this particular indulgence reinforces the legitimacy and spiritual necessity of these practices when properly understood and applied.

On Divine Mercy Sunday, the faithful are invited to meditate on the boundless mercy Christ offers. It's a moment of communal and individual reflection on God's unfathomable love, coupled with the hopeful assurance that no sin places one beyond the reach of divine mercy. This is where the indulgence becomes profoundly personal, touching individual lives through the universal means provided by the Church.

This indulgence also showcases a harmonizing of divine and human components. It allows for the full remission of temporal punishment due to sin, a theological affirmation that God's mercy is active and operative within the living tradition of the Church. By participating in the Divine Mercy devotions, Catholics are drawn into the redemptive mystery of Christ's passion, death, and resurrection, echoing the perpetual call to conversion and sanctity.

In summary, the Divine Mercy Indulgence, while deeply rooted in Catholic tradition, is dynamically relevant to contemporary issues of repentance, forgiveness, and spiritual renewal. Its existence calls upon theologians, canon lawyers, and laity alike to appreciate the depths of Christ's mercy and the Church's role in dispensing that mercy to all who earnestly seek it. Through this indulgence, the Church articulates a timeless truth: in Christ, through the sacraments, and by the authority of the Church, divine mercy remains an ever-available font, cleansing and purifying the repentant heart.

Divine Mercy in Relation to Perfect and Imperfect Contrition

Delving into the profound realm of divine mercy, one encounters the intricate dance between perfect and imperfect contrition. The Catholic Church teaches that God's boundless mercy is ever ready to cloak the penitent sinner, but the nature and quality of that contrition play a definitive role in the efficacy of this divine embrace. At its heart, divine mercy reveals itself not as an unmerited favor indiscriminately bestowed, but rather as a response to the genuine intention behind a sinner's repentance.

Perfect contrition, often described as sorrow for sins rooted in the pure love of God, stands as the ideal. This sorrow transcends mere fear of punishment, reaching into the depths of a profound love for God and regret for having offended Him. Imperfect contrition, by contrast, is fueled predominantly by fear—fear of eternal damnation, temporal punishments, or loss of heavenly rewards. Despite these differences, the Catholic Church holds that even imperfect contrition, when accompanied by the sacrament of confession, renders the penitent eligible for divine mercy.

Historically, the Church's understanding of this dynamic interplay has evolved. Early theological perspectives, notably those influenced by Saint Alphonsus Liguori, elaborated on the necessity of contrition's purity. Liguori's theological framework underscored the importance of the penitent's interior disposition, advocating for a balanced view that acknowledged human frailty while never forsaking the ideal of perfect contrition. Aligning with his teachings, it becomes evident that divine mercy, while infinitely expansive, must be met with a contrite and humble heart.

The nuances of contrition bear significant implications for the sacrament of confession, the wellspring of divine mercy in Catholic practice. Herein lies the tension: the sacrament hinges on the authenticity and quality of the contrite heart presented before God. Perfect contrition, though difficult to attain consistently, allows for a communion with divine mercy even prior to sacramental confession. This potential immediate reconciliation with God highlights the transformative power of perfect contrition as an ideal conduit for divine mercy.

Conversely, imperfect contrition requires the sacrament of confession to bridge the gap between human sinfulness and divine mercy. The sacrament transforms imperfect contrition through the absolution offered by the priest, acting in persona Christi. While fear-based contrition might appear less noble than its perfect counterpart, it still opens the door to divine mercy, emphasizing God's willingness to meet humanity where it is, even amid imperfect motives.

This interplay also touches on deeper theological questions concerning the nature of repentance and divine justice. Can perfect love for God truly reside in human hearts constantly buffeted by fear, doubt, and worldly concerns? Yet, through the lens of divine mercy, even these mixed motives find redemptive potential. By acknowledging the inevitability of human imperfection, the Church underscores God's merciful provision through the sacrament of confession.

The Sacrament of Confession, as it unfolds within the divine mercy framework, becomes not merely a ritualistic observance but a profound encounter with God's grace. By confessing sins with genuine contrition—whether perfect or imperfect—the penitent participates in a transformative process, realigning themselves with God's merciful love. The penitent's journey, facilitated by the sacrament, thereby becomes a testament to the enduring and encompassing nature of divine mercy.

Scriptural accounts further illuminate this relationship. Parables such as the Prodigal Son encapsulate the essence of divine mercy. The returning son, whose contrition may well be deemed imperfect, is nevertheless embraced by a loving father—a metaphor for God's magnanimity. Such narratives offer profound insights into how divine mercy operates on the axis of human contrition, transforming even the most scared and penitent hearts.

Theological discourse sheds additional light on this subject. Debates among scholars often center on whether divine mercy extends to those whose contrition resembles more an acknowledgment of divine retribution than a pure love for God. However, the consensus leans towards recognizing the importance of both forms of contrition within the economy of salvation. Perfect contrition remains the ideal, yet imperfect contrition's acceptance through the sacrament speaks volumes about God's merciful nature.

In exploring the interplay between divine mercy and contrition, one also encounters the concept of grace. Divine grace facilitates true repentance, enabling a movement from fear-based contrition towards a more perfect love of God. Thus, the sacrament of confession, reinforced by divine grace, becomes a pathway to deepen one's relationship with God. This transformative process highlights the dynamic nature of divine mercy in relation to human contrition.

Moreover, ecclesiastical teachings and canonical perspectives affirm the necessity of cultivating a genuine contrite spirit. Canon law underscores the indispensable role of contrition in the sacrament of confession, establishing it as a requisite condition for receiving absolution. Herein lies the intricate balance between divine justice and mercy: while God's mercy is inexhaustible, it requires a heart sincerely striving towards repentance.

Pastoral approaches today recognize the complexities that modern believers face in achieving perfect contrition. The emphasis shifts towards acknowledging the validity of imperfect contrition as a starting point, encouraging the faithful to seek the sacrament of confession. This pragmatic approach not only highlights the Church's pastoral sensitivity but also accentuates the accessibility of divine mercy, irrespective of the penitent's initial disposition.

Through this examination of divine mercy in relation to perfect and imperfect contrition, the interwoven tapestry of God's limitless mercy and human repentance unfolds. The Church's teachings reveal not merely a doctrinal stance but a call to a lived experience of God's infinite love and mercy. While perfect contrition remains the ultimate goal, the recognition and validation of imperfect contrition within the sacramental context affirm God's readiness to meet humanity, redeeming even the most hesitant souls.

Ultimately, the convergence of divine mercy and contrition—perfect or imperfect—draws the faithful into a deeper, more authentic communion with God. It is a journey marked by profound transformation, rooted in the very essence of God's merciful love. This exploration therefore stands as a testament to the enduring hope that, regardless of the nature of one's contrition, the embrace of divine mercy is always within reach, beckoning all towards a greater love and union with the Divine.

Chapter 14: Indulgences and Charity

Interwoven in the rich tapestry of Catholic thought, indulgences and charity emerge as twin pillars that offer a unique pathway to redemption, illuminating the nexus where human frailty and divine grace intersect. Indulgences, often misunderstood, are not mere transactional reprieves from temporal punishment; rather, they embody a profound expression of the Church's treasury of merit, accessible through acts of genuine contrition and charitable endeavors. Concurrently, charity, the greatest of virtues, actualizes the love of Christ through tangible actions, crafting a narrative where faith transcends into works of mercy. Historically, the interplay between indulgences and charity has sparked theological and pastoral contemplation, demanding a delicate balance between justice and mercy. Through indulgences, the Church extends the grace necessary for sinners to amend their lives, while charity cultivates a heart attuned to the needs of others, thus encapsulating the essence of true repentance and spiritual renewal.

How Indulgences and Charity Cover a Multitude of Sins

The intertwining paths of indulgences and charity have long been seen as a means by which the faithful might seek atonement, addressing the residual effects of sin and aiding in reconciliation with God. These practices, deeply rooted in Catholic tradition, serve as vital tools within the broader context of the Church's teachings on sin, forgiveness, and contrition. Understanding their purpose and function requires a close examination, infused with elements of both historical significance and theological nuance.

Indulgences, in the simplest terms, are the remission of the temporal punishment due to sins that have already been forgiven through the Sacrament of Confession. The Church's authority to grant indulgences stems from the belief in the merit of Christ and the Saints, forming what is known as the "Treasury of Merit." This concept holds that the surplus of grace earned by Christ's sacrifice and the holy lives of the saints can aid the faithful in their journey towards purification. By partaking in specific prescribed actions—such as prayers, acts of charity, and pilgrimages—believers can receive these indulgences, lessening their purgatorial burden.

Charity, on the other hand, stands as the greatest of theological virtues. Rooted in the love of God, acts of charity are a direct expression of Christ's commandment to love one's neighbor. Such acts are not only meritorious but also serve to align the faithful with divine will, reflecting their inner conversion in tangible ways. As St. Peter rightly put it, "love covers a multitude of sins" (1 Peter 4:8), implying that the sincerely repentant soul, imbued with love and charity, can find its way back to God's grace.

Historically, the notion of indulgences emerged in the early Church, evolving significantly through the centuries. Initially, periods of rigorous penance were prescribed for grievous sins. Over time, the Church recognized that acts of charity and public service could supplement and even substitute such penances, attainable through an indulgence. The formalization of indulgence practices can be traced to Pope Urban II in the 11th century, especially with his pronouncements during the Crusades, offering plenary indulgences to those who participated.

The intertwining of indulgences and charity was further solidified during the Middle Ages. The Church, recognizing the transactional nature that indulgences sometimes assumed, emphasized that indulgences were not merely "purchased," but rather earned through genuine acts of piety and love. The Council of Trent in the 16th century reaffirmed this stance, condemning the abuse of indulgences while underscoring their spiritual benefits when properly understood and applied.

Engaging in acts of charity often requires a sacrifice of time, resources, or personal comfort, making these actions particularly emblematic of a repentant heart. Donations to the poor, the establishment of hospitals and educational institutions, and personal acts of mercy are just a few ways the faithful have sought to embody charity. Such acts, fueled by love and genuine contrition, serve both the recipient and the giver, knitting the fabric of Christian community closer together.

It is essential to realize that indulgences and acts of charity do not function in isolation; they are inexorably linked to the state of the soul. Without true contrition—whether perfect or imperfect—the pursuit of indulgences can become an empty ritual. Contrition, at its core, involves a sincere sorrow for sins committed and a firm resolution to amend one's life. The grace of God, accessed through the sacraments and manifested in acts of charity, bolsters this contrition, guiding the faithful towards true repentance.

Reflecting on these teachings, one recognizes the delicate balance the Church must maintain. On one hand, indulgences should not be seen as a simple "debit and credit" system where sins are erased through mechanical means. On the other, they must embrace the transformative potential of God's grace. This grace is often channeled through sincere acts of charity—complementing the indulgences and ensuring that the faithful remain focused on their spiritual growth rather than mere ritualistic adherence.

Pope Paul VI, in his 1967 Apostolic Constitution "Indulgentiarum Doctrina," sought to clarify the theology behind indulgences, reiterating their role in the economy of salvation. He emphasized that indulgences are not a form of "cheap grace," but rather an invitation for deeper conversion and genuine acts of love. The document highlighted the vital connection between indulgences, prayer, and works of charity—calling the faithful to a holistic approach to repentance.

Charitable actions often take on a communal dimension within the Church, bringing believers together in a shared mission of mercy and compassion. This communal effort not only amplifies the impact of individual acts but also strengthens the Church's collective witness to the Gospel. By engaging in charity, the faithful demonstrate their solidarity with the suffering and marginalized, embodying Christ's love in a tangible and transformative manner.

In modern times, the concept of indulgences and its relationship with charity might seem archaic to some. Yet, the enduring principles behind these practices remain profoundly relevant. The call to charity is timeless, inviting each generation to renew its commitment to love and selflessness. By participating in acts of charity, contemporary Catholics continue to connect with the rich heritage of their faith, drawing on the wisdom of the past to inform their present actions.

Ultimately, the intricate relationship between indulgences and charity underscores the Church's broader mission of guiding souls towards redemption. These practices, far from being relics of a bygone era, offer valuable pathways for spiritual growth and renewal. They remind the faithful that true repentance involves both an interior transformation and outward expressions of love—both essential in the journey towards eternal union with God.

As Catholic moral theologians, canon lawyers, and devoted practitioners reflect on these teachings, they are called to navigate the delicate balance between doctrine and practice. By fostering a deeper understanding of indulgences and charity, and their capacity to mitigate the temporal effects of sin, they can help guide the faithful towards a more profound experience of God's mercy and grace.

Conclusion

The journey through the labyrinth of sin, contrition, confession, and absolution brings us face-to-face with the intricate dance between divine justice and mercy. Throughout this exploration, the Catholic Church's teachings have served as a compass, pointing us toward a deeper understanding of human frailty and divine compassion. The theological challenges addressed in this work are not mere academic exercises; they are vital to the lived experience of faith and repentance.

Central to our discourse is the delicate tension between perfect and imperfect contrition. While perfect contrition, driven by a pure love of God, represents the ideal, imperfect contrition still holds significant salvific value. This form of contrition, influenced by the fear of divine punishment, underscores the complexity of human motivation. The Church's long-standing recognition of both types of contrition highlights a compassionate approach, offering hope even to those who struggle to achieve the loftier ideal.

Sin, in all its forms, disrupts the harmony between the individual and God. The distinction between venial and mortal sins further complicates the landscape, necessitating a nuanced understanding of their varying impacts on the soul. Venial sins, though less severe, still contribute to spiritual weakness, while mortal sins sever one's relationship with the divine. Understanding these distinctions is crucial for moral theologians and canon lawyers as they guide the faithful.

The Sacrament of Confession stands as a testament to the Church's commitment to reconciliation. The origins and evolution of this sacrament reveal an institution deeply invested in the spiritual well-being of its followers. The role of the priest as a mediator of God's grace is pivotal, providing the penitent with both absolution and spiritual counsel. The journey of the penitent, marked by acknowledgment of sin and sincere repentance, culminates in the joyous embrace of God's mercy.

Yet, the concept of an "unforgivable sin" poses a stark contrast to the overarching theme of mercy. This theological conundrum, rooted in scriptural directives and expounded upon by figures like Liguori, invites profound reflection. The debate surrounding this notion challenges us to consider the limits of divine forgiveness and the gravity of sin that leads to its irrevocability. While the Church teaches that blasphemy against the Holy Spirit remains unforgivable, it also encourages a deeper understanding of this enigmatic sin, urging caution and introspection.

Imperfect contrition, often arising from the fear of God, plays a complex role in the path to reconciliation. The interplay between fear and love in repentance reflects the multifaceted nature of human emotions and motivations. Theological discourse on this topic is replete with debates on the adequacy of contrition motivated by fear alone. Yet, the

Church's teachings affirm that even imperfect contrition can pave the way for divine mercy, illustrating the breadth of God's compassion.

The toughest questions in moral theology often revolve around true repentance and the nature of unforgivable sins. These queries prompt theologians to delve into the essence of human contrition and God's capacity for forgiveness. Real-life case studies of incomplete contrition, both historical and contemporary, provide tangible insights into these abstract concepts. By examining these cases, we gain a better understanding of the practical implications of our theological musings.

Grace emerges as a cornerstone in the discussion of contrition. Divine grace and human free will interact in a dynamic relationship, shaping the penitent's journey toward repentance. This interplay underscores the necessity of divine assistance in achieving true contrition. The Church's teachings on grace emphasize its indispensable role, reminding us that human efforts, while necessary, find their ultimate fulfillment in divine aid.

Ecclesiastical and canonical perspectives provide a structured framework for understanding contrition and confession. Canon Law outlines specific guidelines for the administration of these sacraments, ensuring consistency and doctrinal integrity. Ecclesiastical decrees and teachings further clarify the Church's stance, offering a coherent narrative that supports the faithful in their spiritual endeavors.

Contemporary challenges to traditional notions of contrition and confession demand innovative pastoral approaches. Addressing modern moral dilemmas requires a compassionate and understanding ministry, one that accommodates the complexities of contemporary life. By adapting pastoral practices, the Church can continue to fulfill its mission of guiding the faithful toward reconciliation and spiritual growth.

Divine Mercy, as a facet of God's infinite love, intersects with both perfect and imperfect contrition. The history and practice of Divine Mercy devotion illustrate a profound embodiment of God's willingness to forgive. The Divine Mercy Indulgence, in particular, offers a tangible expression of this mercy, providing the faithful with opportunities to seek and receive God's grace.

The role of indulgences and acts of charity in mitigating the effects of sin cannot be overlooked. These practices, rooted in centuries of tradition, demonstrate the Church's commitment to offering pathways to spiritual renewal. Indulgences, in particular, reflect a nuanced understanding of justice and mercy, bridging the gap between human imperfection and divine holiness.

Ultimately, the themes explored in this work coalesce around the enduring hope found in God's mercy. The intricate theology surrounding unforgivable sins and imperfect contrition serves as a reminder of our perpetual striving for holiness. While we grapple with the weight of our sins and the complexity of our motivations, the Church's sacraments and teachings offer a steadfast beacon of hope and reconciliation.

Appendix A: Appendix

In this appendix, we turn our attention to various key documents and encyclicals that play a significant role in the understanding and practice of the Sacrament of Confession within the Catholic Church. These texts are critical for moral theologians, Roman Catholics, and canon lawyers who are delving into the intricate balance between unforgivable sins and imperfect contrition.

Key Documents

- *Tridentine Catechism*: A vital catechetical text that emerged from the Council of Trent, offering foundational teachings on the sacraments, including penance.
- *Exsurge Domine*: Issued by Pope Leo X, this document was pivotal in addressing the challenges posed by the Reformation, with significant implications for the doctrine of contrition and confession.

- *Reconciliatio et Paenitentia*: Pope John Paul II's apostolic exhortation provides a comprehensive look at the sacrament, emphasizing the roles of contrition and confession in the life of the faithful.

Encyclicals

- ***Misericordia Dei***: An encyclical by Pope John Paul II that elaborates on the sacrament of confession, stressing the need for genuine repentance and the role of divine mercy in the process of absolution.
- ***Redemptor Hominis***: This first encyclical of Pope John Paul II underscores the importance of redemption and the necessity of confession and contrition in the pursuit of salvation.
- ***Veritatis Splendor***: An important text in moral theology by Pope John Paul II that offers insights into the nature of sin, the requirements of true repentance, and the complex interplay between human freedom and divine grace.

These documents and encyclicals provide essential frameworks for comprehending the Church's stance on sin, contrition, and the sacrament of confession. They also help elucidate the theological underpinnings that guide pastoral practices and canon law regarding forgiveness and the necessary conditions for absolution.

For those seeking a deeper understanding of these subjects, the examination of these texts is indispensable. Studying their contents will enrich one's perspective on the intricate doctrines that govern the Catholic Church's teachings on contrition and the sacramental journey of the penitent.

Key Documents and Encyclicals

The Catholic Church has, for centuries, meticulously documented its doctrines, dogmas, and theological deliberations. Central to understanding the sacrament of confession and the related concept of contrition are key documents and encyclicals issued by various Popes and Church councils. These writings provide crucial insights into the development and refinement of Catholic teachings. We will explore some of the seminal documents, noting their contributions and the theological implications they bear on the subject of sin, contrition, and forgiveness.

One of the earliest documents that spoke extensively about confession and contrition is the **Fourth Lateran Council** (1215). This council mandated that every Christian above the age of reason must confess their sins at least once a year. It was a significant step in formalizing the practice of confession, emphasizing its necessity for salvation. The decrees from this council firmly established the Church's stance on the responsibilities of both the confessor and the penitent, outlining conditions under which absolution could be granted. This alignment directed the theological trajectory that would be reflected in numerous subsequent documents and encyclicals.

Moving forward to the Council of Trent (1545-1563), we find extensive doctrinal clarifications in the wake of the Protestant Reformation. The council produced the *Decree on Justification* and the *Decree Concerning the Most Holy Sacrament of Penance*. These decrees reiterated the importance of the sacraments and explicitly addressed the nuances of contrition. Perfect contrition, driven by love for God, was distinguished from imperfect contrition, which arises from fear of divine punishment. Trent's decrees solidified the theology underpinning the sacrament of penance and reaffirmed its indispensable role in the life of the faithful.

Pope Pius X's encyclical *Acerbo Nimis* (1905) addressed the necessity of Christian doctrine and the importance of understanding the sacraments, including penance. Pius X emphasized the role of proper catechesis in ensuring that the laity grasped the significance of confessing sins and the priest's role as an intermediary. This encyclical underscored the Church's commitment to educating its members, ensuring that the sacrament of confession retained its vitality and relevance in modern times.

In the 20th century, Pope Pius XII's encyclical *Mystici Corporis Christi* (1943) provided an extensive look at the Church as the Mystical Body of Christ. This document delved into the interconnectedness of believers and the collective impact of sin and repentance. Pius XII's theological insights highlighted how individual acts of contrition and confession contribute to the well-being of the entire Body of Christ, thereby placing personal piety within the broader context of communal sanctity. It is through these teachings that one can appreciate the ecclesial dimension of penance, where personal reconciliation mirrors the ongoing sanctification of the Church.

Another significant contribution came from Pope John Paul II in his apostolic exhortation *Reconciliatio et Paenitentia* (1984). This exhortation reviewed and renewed the Church's teaching on reconciliation, stressing the dynamism of conversion. John Paul II delved deeper into the personal and social dimensions of sin, underscoring the impact one's sins have on others and the community. His reflections on contrition, both perfect and imperfect, illuminated the necessity of a genuine repentant heart, encouraged the faithful to frequent confession, and highlighted the transformative power of divine grace.

Pope Benedict XVI's encyclical *Spe Salvi* (2007) touched upon eschatological hope and the redemptive nature of suffering and penance. While not exclusively focused on confession, this document addressed the theological underpinnings of repentance and contrition in the context of hope for eternal salvation. Benedict XVI reaffirmed the notion that authentic contrition opens one to the redemptive grace of God, underscoring the sacrament's continuing importance in the journey toward final salvation.

More recently, Pope Francis' apostolic letter *Misericordia et Misera* (2016), issued at the conclusion of the Jubilee Year of Mercy, called for an even more profound focus on mercy within the framework of confession. He urged priests to be more compassionate and understanding, recognizing the struggles of the faithful. This letter is pivotal in understanding the contemporary pastoral approaches to imperfect contrition, as Francis emphasized the church's role in fostering a welcoming environment where penitents feel encouraged to seek God's mercy.

Across these documents and encyclicals, a clear progression and refinement of the Church's understanding of confession, sin, and contrition are evident. Each document builds upon the theological foundations laid by predecessors, responding to the particular challenges and questions of its time. Collectively, they affirm the Church's unwavering commitment to guiding souls toward salvation through the sacrament of confession and the grace of genuine contrition.

As we delve into these documents, it becomes apparent that the Church's teachings on contrition and confession are not static. They evolve, reflecting deeper theological insights and responding to the needs of the faithful. The constant thread, however, is the merciful and redemptive nature of God, which shines through each teaching, encouraging a heartfelt return to Him through the sacrament of confession.

These key documents and encyclicals, therefore, are not just historical artifacts but living testimonies of the Church's effort to assist believers in navigating the spiritual journey of repentance, confession, and reconciliation. They offer moral theologians, Roman Catholics, and canon lawyers a rich tapestry of doctrinal evolution and pastoral wisdom, crucial for understanding the complex interplay between sin, contrition, and divine grace.

Glossary of Terms

Here is a compendium of key terms relevant to the intricate and nuanced subject matter discussed throughout this book. Familiarity with these definitions will aid in a deeper understanding of the complex theological concepts and doctrines presented.

Absolution

The formal release from guilt, obligation, or punishment granted by a priest in the Sacrament of Confession. It signifies God's pardon for sins after contrition and confession.

Contrition

The sincere remorse for having committed sins, accompanied by the resolve to sin no more. Contrition can be either perfect or imperfect, depending on the motive behind the repentance.

Divine Grace

Unmerited favor from God that enables humans to respond to His call to salvation and sanctification. Divine grace plays a crucial role in the process of contrition and forgiveness.

Ecclesiastical

Relating to the Christian Church or its clergy. This term is often used to describe matters or decrees that originate from church authority.

Excommunication

A severe ecclesiastical censure that excludes a person from participating in the sacraments and services of the Christian Church. It is often imposed as a penalty for grave offenses.

Imperfect Contrition

Repentance for sins driven primarily by fear of divine punishment rather than by love for God. While imperfect, it is considered sufficient for receiving the sacrament of confession.

Indulgence

A remission of temporal punishment due for sins that have already been forgiven, granted by the Church under certain conditions. It can be partial or plenary, depending on the degree of remission.

Mortal Sin

A grave violation of God's law that results in the loss of divine grace if committed with full knowledge and deliberate consent. Mortal sins require repentance and confession for absolution.

Penitent

An individual who confesses sins and expresses sorrow for them, seeking forgiveness and absolution from a priest. The journey of the penitent is central to the Sacrament of Confession.

Perfect Contrition

Repentance for sins driven by genuine love for God and sorrow for having offended Him. Perfect contrition, coupled with the intention to confess, can reconcile a sinner with God even before receiving the sacrament.

Remission

The act of absolving or forgiving sins, removing the guilt and eternal punishment associated with them. It denotes the changes in one's standing before God.

Sin

An immoral act considered to be a transgression against divine law. Sins are categorized mainly into venial and mortal based on their severity and implications.

Temporal Punishment

The purification process required to atone for sins, even after they have been forgiven. This can be satisfied through penance, prayer, and acts of charity, or through indulgences.

Unforgivable Sin

Also known as the "blasphemy against the Holy Spirit," it is a sin deemed by scripture and tradition as being beyond the scope of divine forgiveness because of its inherent nature. Theological debates continue regarding its precise definition and implications.

Venial Sin

A lesser sin that does not result in complete separation from God and does not entail eternal damnation. However, it weakens a person's relationship with God and warrants correction.